Best Wishes Mike

Paul Henderson

GOOD LUCK IN YOUR TRYOUTS

SHOOTING FOR GLORY

SHOOTING FOR GLORY

PAUL HENDERSON

WITH MIKE LEONETTI

First published in 1992 by
Stoddart Publishing Co. Limited
34 Lesmill Road
Toronto, Canada
M3B 2T6

Second Printing October 1992

Canadian Cataloguing in Publication Data

Henderson, Paul, 1943-
Shooting for glory

ISBN 0-7737-2646-2

1. Henderson, Paul, 1943-   2. Hockey players —
Canada — Biography.   I. Leonetti, Mike, 1958-
II. Title.

GV848.5.H45A3 1992   796.962'092   C92-094965-7

Typesetting: Tony Gordon Ltd.

Printed and bound in Canada

Stoddart Publishing gratefully acknowledges the support
of the Canada Council, Ontario Arts Council, and Ontario
Publishing Centre in the development of writing and
publishing in Canada.

To my grandchildren,
Brandon, Joshua, and Zachary
P.H.

To my family
M.L.

Contents

Acknowledgements

The authors would like to acknowledge the assistance of the following people: Donald G. Bastian, Adele Boisvert, Carol Bonnett, Michael Carroll, Wanda Goodwin, Eleanor Henderson, Jill Henderson, Michael Lefler, Doug McFadden, Joseph Ramain, and Jim Williamson.

A special thank-you to Rachel Wilson and Nancy Mast for their preparation of the manuscript.

Prologue

Less than a minute to go. The clock in Moscow's Luzhniki Arena was winding down, and the final game remained deadlocked. There would be no overtime, and it looked as if the series might end up tied. Canada's hockey reputation was on the line as it had never been before. With the seconds ticking away I stood up at our bench and called for Peter Mahovlich to come off so I could get on the ice. I don't know why and I can't explain it to this day, but I really felt I could score a goal. Something told me I would do it. I'd had the same kind of feeling when I scored the winning goal in the seventh game.

"Pete! Pete!" I yelled at Mahovlich. I had never called for another player to come off before. It just wasn't done, especially with Harry Sinden coaching. But I didn't care. All I knew was that I had to get on.

"Pete! Pete!" I shouted again. Phil Esposito was out there as usual, but I knew he wouldn't come off the ice. Yvan Cournoyer was on the far side of the rink in the Russian end. There wasn't time for him to come off.

1

"Pete! Pete!" I hollered once more, and this time he heard me. When Mahovlich got to our bench, I jumped over the boards for one last try. . . .

1

The Kid from Lucknow

"Listen up, you guys," my father told the other players in the dressing room between periods of a peewee hockey game. "Just give the puck to Paul and get out of his way. He'll score for you."

I was very embarrassed at the time, but there was no arguing with Garnet Henderson. Dad was over six feet and weighed more than 250 pounds, and when roused he could be quite violent. Even at 15 his strength was legendary. Barely into his teens, he could pick up two 90-pound milk cans in one hand. While working during the winter at the Canadian National Railway station in Lucknow, Ontario, where I grew up, he single-handedly lifted back onto the road a car that had skidded into a ditch. Once, on a dare, he hoisted a 600-pound barrel of salt off the floor and onto a weight scale.

When Dad lost his temper, you didn't want to fool around with him. If someone had challenged him to a fight or crossed him, I'm sure he could have seriously injured that person. Thankfully nothing like that ever happened, nor did he ever hit me or my brother and sisters. Still, even though I was petrified of Dad, I knew I had inherited his drive and determination. A good athlete in his own right, there was no chance for him to achieve the

3

kind of success he craved, since growing up on a farm, marrying at an early age in 1941, and then going off to World War II had taken away many opportunities for him. When he returned from the war, he had a young family to look after, and any plans he might have had for his own future were permanently dashed.

For me, Dad was a difficult man to talk to. Most of our discussions seemed superficial because I was so afraid of him. Dad never talked about his war days. It was a subject you never brought up. While in Germany he survived a mortar shelling that killed eight other men. Dad's jaw was smashed, but a surgeon did a marvellous job of reconstruction. Obviously the memory of that close brush with death was something he wanted to keep deeply buried.

When I think about it now, I have a lot of regret that I never really "talked" to my father. Dad seemed to have a much better rapport with boys five or six years older than I was. The older boys came around because my father was such a great sports enthusiast. He loved fishing and the outdoors, but he spent a good deal of his time coaching baseball and hockey, which was his real passion. Although not the greatest strategist as a coach, his approach certainly appealed to people. He'd take kids anywhere for a game, and I'd tag along as a bat boy or stick boy until I was old enough to play. When any of the players got into trouble, Dad would always help them out, even if the police were involved. Somehow my father always rectified the situation, and the kids really appreciated him for his commitment.

In fact, Dad was a soft touch and quick to help most of the time. As a railway station agent, he would give people their packages without collecting money for them. They would always promise to pay later, but often he ended up owing the cash. Despite the hair-trigger temper, Dad was basically a big-hearted man, and there is no doubt in my mind that his actions taught me to be sensitive to the needs of others.

Still, he could be hard on me. He might have thought I could score a goal on demand, but sometimes there was no pleasing him. Once I scored three goals in a 4-2 win, but after the game he berated me for everything I'd done wrong. When it came to his eldest son, he wasn't very good at dishing out praise.

Even at the beginning my father was absent, although through no fault of his own. My arrival on the scene was quite dramatic. A snowstorm hit the eastern shore of Lake Huron in late January 1943 while my mother, Evelyn, was visiting my father's parents at their farm in Amberly, Ontario. She was pregnant and expecting me any day. So, when Mom went into labour, the closest hospital was in Kincardine, and my grandfather, William Henderson, hitched the horses to a sleigh with the intention of crossing the ice of Lake Huron, a ten-mile trip in the freezing cold of an Ontario winter. About 1,000 yards from the front door my mother gave birth, and when they finally got me into the hospital, I had started to turn blue. Officially I was born on January 28, 1943, in Kincardine, Ontario.

Of course, during all of this my father was overseas with the Canadian army, and I didn't actually meet him until I was three years old. When the war ended, Dad went back to his job as a station agent for the Canadian National Railway. He was posted in various locations, including Port Colborne, Exeter, and Kincardine, before we settled in Lucknow, north of Goderich. All the towns we lived in were typical of rural Ontario during the forties and fifties.

My first memory as a child comes from a time when we were living in Exeter, not far from Stratford. I was about two years old and had a habit of running away from home. To prevent me from wandering off, my mom decided to tie a rope through the belt loops on my pants, with the other end fastened to a post in the backyard. One day during the summer I took off my pants and, bare naked from the waist down, started towards the town's main street. Someone called my mother and told her what I was doing, prompting her to get my toy wagon and follow in pursuit. When she caught up to me, she gave me a spanking, and I distinctly remember crying as she put me into the wagon for the ride home. I can still see the faces of two or three kids as they laughed and pointed at me. Obviously I was one of the first streakers in history!

One of the things I remember most about growing up was that there was never enough money to go around. Any problems we had revolved around the fact that we didn't have money to get the things we wanted. We never lacked for food, but we couldn't afford any luxuries or things I really wanted like sports equipment. My father made pretty good money compared to most, but he was incapable of managing it properly. Anyone can make money, but if you don't handle it intelligently, you can get into trouble quickly. Not surprisingly, we were always in debt.

Despite our poor financial situation, though, we were a close-knit family, and I knew my parents did the best they could. My mother and I have always been particularly close. We've got the same type of personality, which allows us to communicate with each other more easily. She was involved with and concerned about what kind of person I would grow up to be and, like any mother, she wanted what was best for her kids, who eventually, besides me, included brother Bruce and sisters Marilyn, Carolyn, and Sandra. Mom's thoughts back then were geared to the long term, and she has always been a very steadying influence in my life.

When it came to hockey and sports in general, Mom encouraged me to play but worried about the ever-present possibility of injury. Once, when I was playing hockey, I took a shot on the knee, which started to swell and had to be drained. I had a game the day the knee was to be treated. Naturally my mother didn't want me to play, but my father insisted I had to. It wasn't that I didn't want to be in the game; it was just that Dad's dominating personality gave me no choice.

Dad had a very strong constitution. In fact, I don't recall him ever being sick when I was young. Even if he had been, though, his remarkable work ethic would kick in and he'd keep going no matter what. He only slowed down when he suffered a serious stroke at the age of 42. After that he was never the same. The doctors told us he had likely experienced one or two minor heart attacks prior to the stroke, but he was so strong and stubborn that he just fought them off. As proof of his tenacity, even though the doctors only gave him a year at most to live after the stroke, he lived another seven, dying at the age of 49 in 1968.

Garnet Henderson never saw my greatest moment in hockey during the 1972 Canada-Russia series, but he was with me in spirit. Without the encouragement of my father I would have never made it into the NHL. As a coach, though, Dad had his limitations. His temper often got the better of him, especially if his team lost. Once, Bob Hunter, a teammate of mine who liked to get quickly into the offensive zone for my rebounds, went offside several times during one period. Dad started yelling at him, and Bob got so rattled that he wouldn't return to the bench. Instead, he dived into the penalty box on the opposite side of the rink just to avoid my father's wrath.

There was never any doubt in my mind that Dad was quite proud of me, even though he had a hard time expressing it. But what I really needed was someone who could teach me how to play the game properly. My father and most of the other coaches in my early hockey days weren't skill teachers. With no real grasp of the fundamentals of hockey, such as giving or taking passes or stickhandling, I had to get by on raw ability.

I was eight or nine before I learned to skate. I don't recall my first time on the ice, but my father told me I took to skating instinctively. Right away I was fast, which would give me a great advantage as I started to play competitive hockey. Perhaps it helped that I was a fast runner in track and field, but my speed just came naturally.

My first experience with hockey took place in the basement of a Chinese restaurant. Charlie Chin, a Chinese immigrant, opened a restaurant in Lucknow in the 1920s. His sons were excellent hockey players, but their size ruled out any hope of a professional career. When we were kids, though, we'd play ball hockey in the basement of the restaurant. Alan, the youngest Chin, was about a year or two older than I was and had to peel potatoes before he was allowed downstairs to play hockey. Albert Chin, the older brother, was my first coach in peewee, and the family was kind enough to give me my first real hockey equipment, which meant no more department store catalogues as shin guards.

Not unlike many Canadian boys of the time, I spent a great deal of time skating on a pond with friends, particularly Murray Hunter and his brother Bob. We whiled away untold hours playing hockey near the Hunters' house. Many times we froze our toes, but we never seemed to mind because we always had such a good time.

My greatest skill as a hockey player was my ability to skate fast. Once I got the puck and started flying, few players could catch me. My speed allowed me to go around defencemen or to split them and then fire a shot on goal. Soon I started to develop a pretty good shot and goals began to come more easily, thanks to my natural assets.

One of my first thrills in hockey occurred at a peewee tournament in Goderich, where teams from as far away as Winnipeg competed. I scored six goals in one game, which resulted in the first newspaper article with my name in it. After that the other teams started putting somebody on to shadow me, in some cases two people. My father didn't like this at all, and before long he got into pretty intense confrontations with opposing coaches.

I was helped in my development as a hockey player by playing against boys as much as four years older than I was. One year I played three different levels of hockey — bantam, midget, and juvenile. Because we were in a small town there weren't enough players to go around, so I was able to participate at all three levels.

It was as a juvenile, when I was about 15, that I first attracted the recognition of scouts. In a playoff game between Lucknow and Wainfleet I scored 18 goals and added two assists in a 21-6 win. The Wainfleet goalie was so terrified of me that I scored four goals on my first shift. I had a play worked out with our centreman where he would try to flip the puck ahead from the face-off. I jumped on the puck, broke in quickly, and beat the goalie with a shot under the crossbar. My father always instructed me to take my first shot at the goalie's head, so I'd swoop in and rifle a high one as hard as I could. That day everything seemed to go into the net.

My deking ability and finessing moves were limited. I didn't develop these skills, because I was able to outskate most players. I also developed a reputation for my shot, which was hard and accurate. Once, as I began to hurtle down the ice, the goalie left the net and hid behind it. Unlike many players, though, I never used the big windup, the kind you need for a slap shot, because no one ever showed me how to do it properly. I was also afraid of breaking my stick!

My 18-goal game got a write-up in the *London Free Press*, and after hearing about my performance, the professional scouts decided I was worth a look. Three teams showed an interest: Toronto, Boston, and Detroit. The Leafs were pretty arrogant about the whole matter, as if they were doing me a favour. The best scout was Boston's Baldy Cotton, who came to our house and spoke to my father. At the time the Bruins were the worst team in the NHL, and I figured they were my best hope to make the pros. As a result, I decided to attend their junior team training camp the following year in Niagara Falls, Ontario, but I didn't sign the C-Form that bound a player to a team.

In the meantime Jimmy Skinner, the Detroit scout who had shown interest in me, asked, "Why don't you stop over in Hamilton on your way to Niagara Falls and skate with our junior team for a couple of days?" That seemed like a good idea since the Niagara Falls camp started three days after the Hamilton one opened.

As it turned out, I made the Hamilton team, and since that city was closer to home than Niagara Falls, I decided to sign with the Red Wings. Back then, though, my main concern was getting enough playing time, so I opted to play with the Goderich Sailors, the Red Wings' Junior B team. I knew I couldn't get the kind of ice time I needed in Hamilton during my first year. At 16 I was the youngest player on the Sailors and had a pretty good year on a line with Carlo Rossi and Darcy Oliver. We finished fourth in the league but lost in the semifinals to Sarnia. However, the real powerhouse in the league was the team from Saint Mary's, which had a centre named Terry Crisp, who won the scoring title. Terry, of course, went on to coach the Calgary Flames to a Stanley Cup triumph in 1989.

The next season, 1960-61, I was back in Hamilton with the Junior A team. Unfortunately, as I feared, I didn't see much action. As one of the extra forwards, I killed penalties and was assigned spot duty by coach Eddie Bush, who knew I couldn't handle all situations yet but believed I had the potential. When I wasn't with the big club, I played with the Hamilton Bees, the Junior B team in the city. In 12 games with the Bees I bagged 18 goals, which elevated me to the A team in time for the playoffs, where I scored one goal. Saint Michael's took us out in four games straight, though.

Things improved dramatically in 1961-62 when Hamilton won the Memorial Cup. I got plenty of ice time and finished the season with 24 goals in 50 games. Few players get the chance to win a Memorial Cup, and it wasn't easy for us to achieve, either. We beat the Saint Catharines Teepees in six games, overcoming top-notch prospects such as Phil Esposito, Dennis Hull, and Ken Hodge. The Niagara Falls Flyers with J. P. Parise and Terry Crisp took six games to polish off, while Saint Mike's, featuring Rod Seiling, went down in five, the Quebec Citadels in four, and the Edmonton Oil Kings in five. Strangely enough, the Edmonton team was also sponsored by the Red Wings.

Our toughest series was against Saint Catharines. I scored a big goal in the fourth game of that matchup when I took a puck off the wing and came in to beat goalie Roger Crozier, who was trying to cut down the angle. I put the shot right between his legs, and we won the game 4-3, which gave us a 3-1 series lead. In the final in Kitchener against Edmonton I scored a goal in the last game and we won the championship, making the year a very memorable one indeed. I still have a soft spot for that team, which had fine players such as Pit Martin (36 goals), Lowell MacDonald (48 goals to lead the Ontario Hockey Association), and my centreman and our captain, Howie Menard.

Something else that I'll never forget about that Memorial Cup final is the brawl between our coach Eddie Bush and Howie Young, a defenceman for the Detroit Red Wings who had finished that season in Edmonton on the Wings' minor league pro team. Known as hockey's bad boy because of his legendary drinking, Young started cheering for the Oil Kings. At one point he jumped onto the boards, and that's when Bush grabbed him and started a fistfight behind our bench. Despite the ruckus, though, we maintained our composure and went on to capture the junior title.

Eddie Bush was from the old school of coaching. A strict disciplinarian with tough standards, he didn't take guff from anyone. Since I was a pretty headstrong guy, I think I benefitted from Eddie's no-nonsense approach both on and off the ice. For example, I was good at scoring goals, but he taught me the importance of defensive hockey. He told me I had to take care of my own end and stay out of trouble, advice that especially helped me since I wasn't very good at handling the puck back then. Outfinessing people with the puck in my own end was out of the question. I would either shoot the puck out or get it to my centreman as quickly as possible. The lessons weren't lost on me because I became known as a good team player, someone who wasn't averse to backchecking. Bush also taught me to keep my stick on the ice and to correct some skating deficiencies, such as learning to turn both ways equally well and skating backwards with good balance.

Off the ice Eddie had some good advice for me, as well. He was big on projecting a clean-cut appearance, so I had to get a brush cut when I went to Hamilton. Jackets and ties were a must, and when we won the Memorial Cup, Eddie made sure we wore beautiful maroon jackets and matching grey slacks. Since that time, I've always tried to maintain a neat and orderly appearance.

Mind you, I didn't always agree with Eddie. One time, during the Christmas holidays, he made players with families within 100 miles of Hamilton come back and practise while the others could stay at home. Lucknow was just beyond the 100-mile limit, but Bush made me and Gary Doak, who was from Goderich, come back and work out. Only eight of us returned, and Bush skated us hard. I got so mad at him at one practice that I smashed my stick on the net. "You're going to pay for the stick!" Bush roared at me. And I did.

Eddie could be hilarious, as well. At our Memorial Cup celebration banquet he said a few words about each player. When he came to one of our forwards, Earl Heiskala, he couldn't remember his name. Bush said things like, "This big forward from Kirkland Lake was tough and he scored some goals for us," but he couldn't get the name out.

Finally someone in the audience shouted, "Eddie, his name's Earl!"

That brought the house down. Red-faced but unbowed, Eddie kept on as if he hadn't heard anything. Then, finally, he introduced Earl Heiskala to the crowd, which was still rolling in the aisles.

With a Memorial Cup win behind me it was time to think of my future in hockey. In the summer of 1959 I had met Eleanor Alton, who was to become my wife. I first saw her while I was working at Cyril Brown's Lucknow fruit market as a grocery clerk. She came into the store with a friend of hers and, right there and then, I was smitten by the sight of a slim, fifteen-year-old girl with beautiful brown hair. Eleanor and her girlfriend were examining lettuce when I made my approach.

"Can I help you?" I asked.

"We're looking for some lettuce," Eleanor replied.

"Don't touch that stuff," I said, immediately taking charge. "Wait right here."

I walked quickly to the back of the store where I knew we had a fresh supply of lettuce in cases. After opening at least eight boxes, I found two huge heads of lettuce. Working fast, I cleaned them off, then checked my own appearance. The Elvis Presley look was hot back then, so I slicked my hair back and put up my shirt collar. When I returned to the main part of the store, holding the heads of lettuce, I tried to act as cool as I could. Of course, I was about as smooth as sandpaper, but still managed to strike up a conversation with Eleanor and her friend. Before long I got the telephone number I was after.

For our first date I drove out to her father's farm, where it was harvest time and she was doing the chores. To be specific, she was milking the cows. I offered to help her out but had trouble picking up a filled milk can. Eleanor lifted it with little effort. I also noticed that her well-worn jeans had a revealing slit running from knee to hip. Beauty and strength, I thought. Not bad.

After she finished the chores, Eleanor washed up and changed clothes so that we could drive into Goderich. I wanted to show her off, and on a Friday night everybody would be out. With a beauty like Eleanor sitting beside me in my father's 1955 Ford, I felt like a million bucks and decided to prove I was a big spender.

"Would you like a hot dog, fries, and a Coke?" I asked.

"That would be nice," she replied with a smile.

We pulled into Pete's Hot Dog Stand, and I got out of the car and ordered two foot-long dogs, two large fries, and two giant Cokes. As I walked back to the Ford, I was feeling pretty cocky about everything, but when I handed Eleanor her hot dog, fries, and Coke, I let go an instant too soon. The whole works tumbled onto her white linen skirt. I was so embarrassed that I wanted to dive under the car. But Eleanor has always had a terrific sense of humour. She must have; she agreed to see me again!

I had another tough first moment with Eleanor's parents. I was playing Junior B hockey in Goderich, and we convinced them to come see me play a game. Since they had a farm, all the chores had to be done before they could leave, which meant they arrived a little late. I just happened to look up and notice them coming in. They had seats near the blue line. As Eleanor's mother sat down, she looked up and the puck came flying over the boards, catching her right in the mouth and forcing her to leave the game to get stitched up. What a way to introduce yourself to your future mother-in-law!

On our second date I told Eleanor I was going to marry her. She laughed at me and thought I was joking. But I was dead serious. Over the next few years I soon learned that Eleanor had brains to go along with all that beauty and strength, both physical and spiritual. In November 1962 we were finally married, and it's been quite a partnership for thirty years.

But that summer after the Memorial Cup victory in 1962 I had a lot of soul-searching to do with Eleanor. We talked about our plans and how we wanted to live. Our parents had done a great job of instilling us with good values. They had given us so much, but like any other young couple, we had dreams of an easier life than our parents had. We had visions of a house with a white picket fence and a nice car in the driveway, no doubt the standard early sixties aspirations.

So I started looking at my options. In spite of the demands hockey imposed on me I had always been a good student and could get good marks when I wanted to; it was just that I was more interested in playing sports. Since I knew I'd have little time for homework between hockey and a part-time job, I usually sat near the front of the class and took detailed notes. I did all of my work at school and rarely if ever did any at home, even throughout high school. Somehow I got by with my notes and listening skills, but finding time to do school work after going to Hamilton to play junior hockey was even more difficult. Still, I was confident that if I devoted myself to getting an education, I could be a top student.

There was a schoolteacher in Lucknow who I thought had the perfect job. He taught history and physical education, which seemed like a terrific combination for me, since I really loved history and could keep my hand in athletics. I knew this type of job would never make me wealthy or give me celebrity status, but it would be secure, which would be enough for me and Eleanor. She had always enjoyed sharing in my hockey endeavours,

but she encouraged me to go to university and work towards a teaching career. I was ready to tell the Red Wings
I was going to pack it in.

However, a conversation with my father changed my
mind. "If you quit now," he said to me, "it'll drive you
crazy until the day you die, wondering if you could have
made it." Those words made a big impression on me.
Could I live with these questions and doubts? In my
mind there was no uncertainty that I could play pro
hockey. My father and I probably spoke more at this turning point in my life than we ever had before. He was
worried that I was going to quit the game just when the
ultimate goal of the NHL was so close. After discussing
the matter with Eleanor, I decided to give myself two
years to make the NHL. If I didn't succeed within that
time frame, I'd return to school and work towards becoming a teacher. Doing it that way would remove any
doubts and I could get on with my life.

At this point Eddie Bush sat down and gave me a talk
that set me on the right course to becoming an NHLer.
"You have the skating ability, the strength, and the desire
to play in the NHL," he said. "You've got to hone your
skills now. Let others play tough and get into fights. You
go out and score goals. Play aggressively, but don't fight.
Use your speed and shot to get goals. Fighters are a dime
a dozen. Goal scoring will get you into the NHL."

I listened carefully to what Bush said. He had played in
the NHL briefly for Detroit in the early forties and had
won three OHA titles with Guelph. Eddie had coached
players like Rod Gilbert and Jean Ratelle and knew what
he was talking about. Thanks to him I became totally focused on playing my game.

During my final season of junior hockey, 1962-63, I
scored 49 goals in 48 games to lead the OHA. I worked

very hard at all aspects of the game but concentrated on scoring goals. My roommate, goaltender Buddy Blom, was a big help. We would stay after practice so I could work on releasing my shot quickly. If you can get off a shot just a split second sooner, it can mean a lot more goals.

We didn't have as good a team as the previous season when we won the Memorial Cup. Saint Mike's knocked us out of the playoffs with relative ease. I missed the postseason due to strep throat, but I don't think I would have had much impact on the result. My junior career was over and I was ready to move on.

Even in grade five I had a fixation on the NHL. Quite early in life I started working on my autograph in the hope that one day people would ask me to write my name on a piece of paper. A couple of years later in grade seven after I didn't do my homework the school principal wanted to know why I wasn't prepared.

"It's not going to matter," I told him rashly. "I'm going to play in the NHL."

The principal laughed and quite rightly pointed out that there were only 120 players in the whole league at that time. "You're never going to make it," he chided.

If anything, this conversation gave me incentive, because I took an "I'm going to show him" attitude. I thrived on competition and challenge. The principal merely fuelled my desire to make it in big-time hockey. I knew I still had plenty to learn, but there was no way I was going to be intimidated. Hockey would give me the kind of lifestyle I desired. No question.

Like most boys in Canada of my generation, I first dreamed of playing in the NHL by listening to Foster Hewitt on the radio every Saturday night. My father and I listened and later watched the games on television together, which helped us picture the ultimate goal of Paul Henderson in the NHL. I didn't have a favourite team, but I admired Gordie Howe and Maurice "Rocket" Richard because they were right wingers like me. They had made it. I wanted to show everybody that the kid from Lucknow could make it, too.

2

Turning Pro

Beer, pizza, and long bus rides. Big time. Well, not quite. Those are the things I remember most about playing in the American Hockey League. The guys in the AHL were a close bunch, without the kind of cliques common in the NHL. Many of the players knew they were never going to make it big-time again, so they decided to enjoy themselves and act like good old boys. The veteran players went out of their way whenever possible to teach me some of the finer points of the game. I never got much advice in the NHL, which was far too competitive to share tips with a rookie. But the AHL was a different story.

Hank Ciesla was one of those AHL veterans I remember most. "Never forget us defencemen," Hank would tell me on one of those gruelling road trips. "Always try to play a two-way game and we'll look out for you." For a guy barely out of his teens with his first taste of freedom and a tendency to charge ahead with reckless abandon, having vets like Hank Ciesla, Pete Geogan, Adam Keller, and Claude Laforge watch over you was a source of great relief.

And the stories! Defenceman Warren Godfrey, especially, had a million of them, and when we weren't play-

ing cards on those seemingly endless bus hauls between
Rochester, Springfield, Quebec City, Cleveland, Buffalo,
and Hershey, he'd keep us in stitches with one rib tickler
after another. They were all characters in the AHL, a
minor league that boasted tough, hard-nosed men like
Don Cherry, Fred Glover, Bep Guidolin, Al Arbour, Willie
Marshall, and Bill Sweeney. Baz Bastien, our general manager on the Pittsburgh Hornets, was always pulling fast
ones on us, particularly green kids like me. Once, while
we were unwinding with a few beers and something to
eat after a game, I took a look at Baz's plate and saw an
eye staring up at me. The guys were trying hard not to
burst out laughing. They knew Bastien had a glass eye.
All I could think of was that Baz had some pretty pecu-
liar tastes in food.

I knew I needed to spend some time in the minors. In
fact, in my last year of junior, after I recovered from a
bout of strep throat, I got called up unexpectedly by Detroit when Floyd Smith was injured and Bruce
MacGregor's father died. The Red Wings told me to report to Toronto for a weekend home-and-home series
with the Leafs. Before the first game my father told me,
"Get out there, son, and show them what's what." Dad
felt this was the big moment we'd worked so hard to
achieve. He wanted me to make the NHL sit up and take
notice. Did I ever! Sort of. Initially, though, all I did was
warm the bench until the second period when coach Sid
Abel finally gave me the call.

I hurled myself over the boards, my father's words
echoing in my mind, and within eight seconds found myself elbowing the Leafs' Dick Duff in the head. Duff threw
off his gloves and away we went. I couldn't believe it!
Here I was wrestling my hero Dick Duff to the ice. I
could have really hammered him, too, since I had a head-

lock on him. But neither one of us was really a fighter, and soon the referee managed to separate us.

I got two minutes for elbowing and five minutes for fighting and sat in the penalty box while the other Leaf players, guys like Bobby Baun, Eddie Shack, Allan Stanley, and Tim Horton, called me every name in the book and threatened me with all kinds of unmentionable retaliations involving their sticks. Luckily for me, the Leafs got a penalty, and when my sentence was over, Abel motioned me back to our bench. As soon as I got there, I dived in, overjoyed that I didn't encounter any of the previously mentioned players.

The next night, back in Detroit, Abel gave me my first shift well into the first period. I was out against big Frank Mahovlich, who managed to get past me on the outside. But not for long. I wheeled around and gave him a two-handed whack with my stick, poleaxing him. He went down like a felled ox, then popped back up again, ready to tear my head off. This time the referee got between us before the fists started flying. Naturally I got a penalty for slashing, even though I'd only been out on the ice for ten seconds, maybe less.

After the incident in Toronto the night before and now this, the Leafs wanted to lynch me. But luck was on my side again. Just as my penalty ended, an offside was called and I returned to our bench, where Sid Abel demanded, "For God's sake, Henderson, can't you stay on the ice?" Not surprisingly, he didn't send me out again. But I must have collared some kind of record. Nine minutes of penalties in less than twenty seconds of ice time. No mean feat!

Impatient as I was to get to the NHL, it didn't take me long in my first pro camp to realize I had a lot of rough edges, something no doubt pretty evident to the Red

Wings after my juggernaut debut with the big team at the
end of the previous season. There were a lot of familiar
faces from Junior A in that first camp in 1963. Like me,
Larry Jeffrey, Lowell MacDonald, Pit Martin, and Bob
Wall were all hopefuls. So, even though I was probably
the fastest skater at the camp, the Red Wings sent me
down to Pittsburgh.

The AHL was a good league during the 1960s. If an
AHL team played an NHL team in that era, the difference
might be a goal. The Rochester Americans, Don Cherry's
team in the AHL, were easily a match for weaker NHL
teams like Boston and New York. With only 120 jobs
available in the big league, some very talented people
played in the AHL. I think seven or eight players on each
AHL team could have replaced the bottom three or four
players on almost all the NHL teams. Many of the players
in the AHL tried to find a niche that would get them into
the NHL. Some found it while others became career
minor leaguers. I preferred playing in the AHL at that
time because there were so many borderline NHLers in
the league who were seasoned professionals. They knew
how to play the game and provided me with the environ-
ment I needed to improve.

The Hornets had a nice mix of older vets and younger
players like myself. I got along well with playing coach
Vic Stasiuk, who had had a long NHL career with Chicago, Boston, and Detroit. He gave me plenty of work,
including power plays and penalty killing. The vets appreciated my style because I was aggressive and would
use my speed to get the puck out of our end. I played on
a very good line with winger Yves Locas, who led the
AHL that year with 40 goals, and centre Art Stratton, who
topped the league with 65 assists. I learned a lot by
watching Art handle the puck. Later, he made it back to

the NHL with the Pittsburgh Penguins and the Philadelphia Flyers.

Life in Pittsburgh wasn't too tough to adjust to. Eleanor and I rented an apartment in a building where an older couple, the Dabneys, took us under their wing. When I was on the road, they looked in on Eleanor and our young daughter Heather. The city had just built the Igloo (now called the Civic Arena), which gave us a new facility to work in. I was happy in Pittsburgh and wanted to spend the season there, but the Red Wings ran into problems in November and I got called up to the big team.

I asked the Red Wings to send me back to Pittsburgh so I could spend Christmas with my family, which would always be a priority for me. The Red Wings understood and let me return for a couple of weeks. Early in the new year, 1964, I returned to Detroit and said goodbye to the minors forever. My AHL career consisted of 38 games, 10 goals, and 24 points.

There was a lot of pressure playing in the old six-team league. Prior to expansion in 1967, you could never take a night off for fear of losing your job. A couple of bad games and you might find yourself back in the minors. Every player went through the same anxiety until they established themselves as NHLers. Management used this fear as leverage to get you to do what they wanted. The front office held all the cards and ruled a player's life completely. This all changed with expansion, but at the time I responded well to pressure. I knew it was my chance to make it with the Red Wings.

The NHL players were much more cliquish than the minor league guys. Not many reached out to make us feel welcome. Bruce MacGregor and his wife, Audrey, were the exceptions. Eleanor and I struck up a friendship with them, and we got along so well that we decided to live in

Windsor, where Bruce and Audrey resided. Bruce had only been in the league two or three years but was already a vet. As I look back, I now know I should have tried to help out rookies the way Bruce did. But in those early days fear of losing your job was the number one concern, and competition was cutthroat.

Play in the NHL during the mid-1960s was pretty intense. The hitting could be fierce at times, but the players all had respect for one another. There were few if any cheap shot artists in the league. My real introduction to the league was a freight train named Leo Boivin. I broke up the middle with my head down, looking for a pass. Boivin, who played for Boston, hit me with a check that just about killed me. I felt as if he broke every bone in my body. I'm sure the hairs on my arm hurt for two days! It was a clean hit, though, and Leo said, "Welcome to the NHL, son." I made up my mind right there that I was never going to get hit like that again.

Since I wasn't ready for full-time duty, Sid Abel used me primarily as a penalty killer. In 32 games I scored three goals and made three assists, and in 14 playoff games I added two more goals and three assists. The Red Wings had finished fourth in the six-team league and upset Chicago in seven games to advance to the finals against Toronto. Pretty heady stuff for a rookie.

We had the Maple Leafs down 3-2 in games with the sixth game at the Detroit Olympia. I scored a breakaway goal on Johnny Bower to tie the game 1-1 early in the second period. We had a 3-2 lead late in the second period when the Leafs' Billy Harris tied it on one of his few shifts of the game. After a scoreless third, Toronto's Bobby Baun scored one of hockey's most memorable goals, playing on a broken leg. This forced a seventh game back in Toronto, which we lost 4-0. I remember crying like a baby after the game. It still ranks as one of the greatest disappointments in my life. Imagine being on a Stanley Cup winning team as a rookie! The only thing that helped ease the pain was the playoff bonus money.

One of my teammates during my first year in Detroit was Terry Sawchuk. I only played with "Ukey" for the last part of the 1963-64 season, but there is no doubt in my mind that Terry was the greatest goalie of that era. Like most goaltenders, Terry was a little different from the rest of the players. However, in the big games you wanted Sawchuk backstopping you. He played some outstanding hockey for the Red Wings. I remember talking to him as we were coming home on the bus after the fifth game in Toronto during the finals. We had a 3-2 series lead. "If we win the Stanley Cup," Terry told me, "I'm going to throw my skates into the garbage and call it quits." We lost the series to the Leafs, but Terry wasn't quite ready to pack it in. Toronto drafted him, and he tended goal there for another three years, playing a key role in the Leafs' amazing Stanley Cup win in 1967.

I felt badly for Bill Gadsby after the Toronto loss. Bobby Baun's overtime winner had deflected off Gadsby's stick and sailed over Sawchuk's shoulder. Gads played 20 years in the league with Chicago, New York, and Detroit, and he had just missed his best chance to win a Stanley Cup. Gads lasted so long because he was a great hockey player. He loved playing with me because he knew I was fast enough to dig out a puck in our own end, which allowed Gads to stand up at the blue line and belt guys. He was big and tough and knew how to use his elbows effectively. "When they dump the puck in on my side," he'd tell me, "You go and get it and I'll hammer the winger. Don't worry. They won't get near you." With protection like that, who could go wrong?

The following season, 1964-65, was my first full year in the NHL. I played in all 70 games, racking up 21 points, including eight goals. I was the fourth right winger behind Gordie Howe, Bruce MacGregor, and Floyd Smith. My ice time was limited, though. I was still killing penalties and learning to contribute defensively when I got my occasional shift. That season we ended up in first place with 87 points, but this time Chicago, and a hot Bobby Hull, pulled off the upset in seven games.

Detroit had a pretty solid team in those days, with guys like Gordie Howe, Norm Ullman, Alex Delvecchio, Marcel Pronovost, and Ted Lindsay. They seemed to accept newcomers like myself and Pit Martin, even though Pit and I were not passive rookies who would take much from the older guys. In fact, we were probably a little too cocky for our own good. They let us get our way just enough, although there was no way to escape the rookie initiation — an extensive body shave. Their revenge was complete when they shellacked my body after the shave. Once this ritual was over, though, you did feel part of the team.

The other thing I felt I needed to do to be a full-fledged Red Wing was learn how to drink. It took me my entire rookie season before I could begin to keep up with some of the players on the team. Sometimes Pit and I would get groggy with beer twice in one day. When on the road, we would go for a couple after practice to help swallow down some lunch. Then we'd get some sleep, go back, and meet the same guys for drinks and dinner. I couldn't believe how much NHL players drank.

If there was one person I idolized on the Red Wings, it was Howe. He was my hero when I was growing up. I'd sit and watch him play hockey as if he were a god. Gordie was just a big kid who loved to play the game. He was never affected by his stature in the league. He took it all in stride and just came to play hockey. His strength was truly amazing, and he used it not only in hockey but to play golf, as well. He could drive a golf ball a mile. One legend about Howe that is the absolute truth — he was the toughest, meanest player in the NHL. He took crap from nobody.

Gordie was terrific to me and my family. He really liked Heather, my eldest daughter, and always had time for her. When I was traded to Toronto, I knew I'd have to play against Gordie, since he played right wing and I was by then a left winger. I had seen what Gordie had done to other players when they were traded by the Red Wings. He'd give them some cruel shots, so I was definitely worried about how he'd treat me as an opponent. On my first shift against Gordie as a Maple Leaf he asked me how I was doing and how my family was adjusting to the trade. His concern seemed genuine, much to my relief. Just the same, I never took my eyes off him. Still, as far as I can remember, Gordie never singled me out for his special treatment.

Gordie had his own way of dishing out punishment. One night, while with the Leafs, Toronto defenceman Mike Pelyk roughed it up with Gordie. When Pelyk came back to the bench, I tried to warn him. "Watch out for the big guy," I told him. Being young and inexperienced, Pelyk didn't take the advice to heart. Later in the game Gordie introduced Pelyk to his stick. Five lost teeth and over thirty stitches later, Pelyk learned you didn't mess with Mr. Howe!

Ted Lindsay rejoined the Red Wings for the 1964-65 season. He had been retired for the past four years after ending his career with the Chicago Blackhawks. Ted had played on four Stanley Cup Red Wing teams in the 1950s.

He was a gritty little hockey player who feared no one even though he couldn't have weighed more than 160 pounds. Upon his return, Ted was as feisty as ever. One night against Toronto Ted got into a scrap with Dickie Moore, who ironically enough was also making a comeback with the Leafs after his great career with the Montreal Canadiens. A lot of time may have gone by, but these two veteran gladiators hadn't forgotten their rivalry. Moore smacked Lindsay in the nose, and off they went. In the six-team era you battled your opponent with all you had. At the age of 40 Lindsay accumulated 173 minutes in penalties.

Goaltender Roger Crozier joined the Red Wings in the 1964-65 season. He was voted rookie of the year and was named a first-team all-star. Roger was a smallish, acrobatic goalie noted for making dazzling saves. How he did it, I'll never know. Roger was always a bundle of nerves, but who could blame him with Bobby Hull taking aim for one of his 100-mile-per-hour slap shots? This was still in the era when goalies didn't wear masks. Just thinking about a Hull blast heading my way makes me shiver. No wonder Bobby led the league in goals seven times.

In 1965-66 an overabundance of right wingers and an injury to Ron Murphy gave me an opportunity to be a left winger on a line with centre Norm Ullman. I scored 22 goals and added 24 assists. Twenty goals in the six-team NHL was an accomplishment, especially for a young player like myself. I owe much of my success to Normie, who was a pleasure to play with. A great playmaker, he would feed me the puck on the wing, and I knew I could always find him in the slot. "Try to beat the defencemen to the outside," Normie would instruct, "and I'll try to get you the puck." After a while we worked pretty effectively. Ullman was a dogged forechecker and had great stamina. We often played against the top lines in the league centred by people like Henri Richard and Stan Mikita. Basically I stayed as Normie's left winger for the rest of my NHL career. Playing next to a Hall of Famer never hurts!

That season the Red Wings dropped to fourth place, finishing with 74 points, sixteen behind first-place Montreal. We upset second-place Chicago in six games, putting us into the finals against the Canadiens. Things got off to a great start and we jumped out to a 2-0 lead by winning twice at the Forum. Then we proceeded to blow the next four in a row, losing the Stanley Cup in six games!

Montreal had a great hockey team, but we lost the series because we had no discipline. Instead of practising during the playoffs, we hung out at the racetrack and in bars. Some of the older guys on the team should have stood up and said, "Let's start behaving ourselves," but they didn't. To put it bluntly, our coach Sid Abel lost control of the team.

The Canadiens, on the other hand, wanted to win more than we did. They stayed disciplined both on and off the ice. The Canadien players made sure they got to bed after a beer or two. Some Red Wings were more familiar with the bars in Detroit than with their beds. As if that wasn't enough, Detroit owner Jim Norris had a picture taken of himself and some of the Red Wings smoking cigars after our second win. They acted as if we'd already won the Cup. When the newspapers published the picture, Montreal coach Toe Blake got his hands on it and put it up in the Canadiens' dressing room. No doubt the photo proved to be a great motivator.

The series ended on a controversial note when Henri Richard scored the winning goal in overtime. I was on the ice at the time, and it honestly looked to me as if he put the goal in with his hand. The referee could have ruled either way, but the call in those prevideo days went against us, and the Canadiens took the Cup right in the Olympia. That game will always be a sour note in my career. To be so close and yet fall so short. It still rankles.

Prior to the 1966-67 season I had to sign a new contract with the Red Wings. In those days most players signed their contract during training camp. I decided to ask around to see what the other players thought I should ask for in terms of a raise. Most of them thought $2,500 would be more than reasonable, but that didn't seem right to me. Originally I had signed for $7,000 and received only $1,500 as a signing bonus. I don't know why exactly, but I went into Sid Abel's office and asked for a $7,000 raise. I was probably as surprised as he was when the figure popped out of my mouth. Abel cursed, said I was crazy, and told me to get out. But I dug in my heels.

The dickering continued all through training camp. When owner Jim Norris came into town, he wanted the issue settled before the first home game. If the first game had been on the road, I might have had to sit out, but as things developed, I signed the day of the first regular-season game. I think the Red Wings gave me what I asked for because they wanted a quick start after going to the finals the previous year. Nevertheless, Abel tried to beat me into submission in what became a war of nerves. Back then no one had an agent, but I stuck to my guns, anyway, which was an achievement in those days before the advent of Alan Eagleson. It's hard to believe we were quibbling over several thousands back then, not hundreds of thousands as is the case today.

The 1966-67 season wasn't a memorable one for both me or the Red Wings. I managed 21 goals but played in only 46 games, and the team missed the playoffs. I might have scored 35 or 40 goals if I could have played the full 70 games, but I missed nearly a third of the season with various injuries, including torn chest muscles. I also developed a breathing problem and eventually had to go to Arizona for a couple of weeks to clear it up. As I got better, though, the Red Wings grew sicker.

A big loss for the Red Wings was an injury to Doug Barkley, whose career ended when he took a stick in the eye. The severity of the injury was never understood and it cost Detroit a top defenceman. I think Barkley might have won the Norris Trophy one day. Also gone were Marcel Pronovost, who was traded to Toronto, and Bill Gadsby, who retired. Detroit's defence totally collapsed. As I learned many times in my career, you can't win without good people behind the blue line.

By the start of the 1967-68 season Detroit's defence consisted of a couple of inexperienced young players and a few solid journeymen. The Red Wings gave up a league high of 257 goals, even more than any of the six expansion teams. But on the way to the bottom of the East Division Detroit pulled off one of hockey's biggest trades.

My life changed significantly on March 3, 1968, when the Red Wings dealt me to the Maple Leafs. Toronto also received centre Norm Ullman and right winger Floyd Smith. In return Detroit got left winger Frank Mahovlich, centre Peter Stemkowski, rookie Garry Unger, and the rights to defenceman Carl Brewer.

I felt totally betrayed. I had been with the Red Wing organization since my junior days in Hamilton, and being the optimistic person that I was and still am, I assumed I'd play my entire career in Detroit. When you're young and have never been traded before, you tend to be naive about the realities of pro hockey. Looking back at it now,

coming to Toronto was the best thing that ever happened
to me. Nonetheless, being traded hurt. Detroit had been
good to me. Toronto had been good for Mahovlich. He
had legions of fans who had followed his career since his
junior days with Saint Mike's. Realistically Frank had to
leave the Leafs to get his game back together, and did he
ever later when he was traded to Montreal.

Leaf coach and general manager Punch Imlach came
down to Detroit with his sidekick King Clancy to sign the
papers completing the deal. We were playing the Canadiens that night and I happened to get into a fight with
John Ferguson. I'd taken out Ferguson on a good hit in
the corner. He came back and suckered me afterwards in
a face-off. I ended up with a black eye, which is about as
well as I did in any of my fights. In his book *Hockey Is a
Battle* Imlach said he was impressed with my aggressive-
ness, something Punch felt was lacking among the Leafs.
Punch had once told me he'd get me to Toronto someday,
but I never dreamed it would actually happen.

Imlach had a reputation for being a tough coach. Luckily I was able to get along well with him. If you kept your
mouth shut and did what Imlach asked you to do, most
of the time you had no problems with him. My junior
coach Eddie Bush always told me not to fight with the
coach; there was no way you could win, especially back
in the sixties. But one thing I always respected about
Punch: he played straight with me.

On occasion Imlach would show his appreciation, although he usually did so in private. One night after a
game in Saint Louis he came up to me when everyone
was gone and thanked me for playing under difficult circumstances. I was in a great deal of pain because of torn
chest muscles, but I scored one goal and had an assist in
a 3-2 win. He knew I was hurting and wanted to show

me he understood. However, he had problems handling other players. With a sky-high ego and an inclination to be overly superstitious, he often coached on hunches, which made it hard to agree with him a lot of the time. His superstitions could be pretty amusing sometimes. He always had a lucky suit when the team was on a roll, and every season, like clockwork, he sent Jim Pappin down to the minors.

Despite my initial reservations, I soon found myself at home in a Maple Leaf uniform. Even though I'd had no favourite team as a kid, Maple Leaf Gardens was a special place. The first time I entered the building it felt as if I'd died and gone to heaven. You could feel the tradition as you walked the halls and corridors. The air hummed with history. Being on television a lot more was an added bonus, since I thrived under the spotlight. The thought of being on *Hockey Night in Canada* every Saturday was a dream come true. I knew there would be pressure, but that's when I played my best hockey.

Unfortunately the Leafs were like the Red Wings in many ways. Although Toronto had won the Stanley Cup the year before I arrived, the team was in an obvious state of transition. The rising power in the league was the Boston Bruins, followed by the New York Rangers, while the Montreal Canadiens always remained solid. I felt it would be up to management to rebuild the team around players like Dave Keon, Ron Ellis, Norm Ullman, Mike Walton, and a group of neophyte defencemen. Young rear guards like Jim Dorey, Pat Quinn, and Mike Pelyk would give the Leafs a nice blend of youth and experience, as did Rick Ley, Brad Selwood, Jim McKenny, and Brian Glennie later on.

Even though we came close, the Leafs still missed the playoffs in 1968. I had 11 points in 13 games for Toronto to finish the season, playing on a line with the other ex-Wings, Norm Ullman and Floyd Smith. The next season, 1968-69, was my first full year in Toronto, and we bounced back to finish in fourth place with 85 points. I started to feel comfortable in Toronto and stayed fairly healthy.

In the playoffs we were pitted against the Bruins, who humiliated us in Boston 10-0 and 7-0. We didn't stand a chance against the new league powerhouse and were quickly dispatched in four games straight. Punch Imlach was fired immediately after the final game. The way he was let go made me realize just how ruthless the hockey business could be. The owners could do whatever they wanted, and some of them had very little respect for people as human beings. At the end of the next season I got a personal taste of management insensitivity and short-sightedness.

In 1969-70 the Leafs finished last in the East Division with a mere 71 points. I had a less than satisfying year, scoring only 20 goals and 42 points, significant declines from the previous season. I played the entire season with a groin problem, but the most irritating part of the whole year was management's refusal to give me time off to let my injury heal properly. By the end of the season, my right thigh was an inch and a half bigger than my left because I was basically skating on one leg. My groin was never the same, which in turn affected my speed. I was stupid not to tell coach Johnny McLellan to let me get better. Today no player would risk further injury that way. Trainers have much better control over such situations, and the powers that be in hockey are more aware of the dangers of skating an improperly healed player.

That summer the Leafs sent me a new contract in the mail, offering a raise of $1,500. Leaf general manager Jim

Gregory and King Clancy called me about the contract. I just about went through the roof when they told me they didn't think I deserved much of a raise since my production had declined. I reminded them that I had played my guts out in a great deal of pain because of the groin injury. There were a lot of games I shouldn't even have dressed for.

"Oh, we forgot," they said.

"You forgot?" I fumed.

"We'll go back and think about the offer again," Gregory replied.

They came back with a better proposal, but the damage had been done. My whole attitude changed. Hockey had become a business, and management was only interested in numbers. The harsh reality was that the game wasn't going to look after me or my family. Only Paul Henderson could do that.

The Leaf team I joined had a few players left from the group that had won four Stanley Cups in six years. George Armstrong, who we called the Chief, captained the Leafs to these championships. He had a way of keeping you loose and knew when to have fun and when to be serious. On the ice he was all business; off it he was quite a cutup.

The Chief roomed with Johnny Bower, a goalie who hated anyone scoring on him, even in practice. Some goalies dogged it in practice, but not Johnny. Once he was between the pipes, Bower acted as if he were in playoff overtime, whatever the situation. Bower's sleeping habits were different from those of the Chief. Armstrong liked to sleep with all the windows open with just a sheet to cover him, even in the winter. Bower wasn't comfortable without long johns, a sweater, blankets, and a hat when he finally hit the hay. They made a strange pair.

Another great Leaf was Dave Keon, who was easily one of the most finicky people I've ever seen, especially when it came to his equipment. Everything had to be just so. He was a perfectionist by nature and lived for hockey. Davey was also a pretty good golfer, but he preferred to practise as much as he actually played. On the first day of camp Keon would be in such great shape that he'd skate away from the rest of us, as if he were ready for the seventh game of the finals! You could see why he was such a great competitor. It seemed as if he always saved his great games for the playoffs. Davey was a leader by example, but was never one for making too many speeches in the dressing room.

Johnny McLellan took over as coach of the Leafs in 1969-70. He was one of the nicest people you'd ever want to meet. Probably too nice to be a coach in the NHL. People took advantage of him. To be fair, Johnny didn't inherit a good team, a fact brought home even more when Tim Horton was traded to the New York Rangers.

Tim was a great guy, a man's man. You felt so much better with him out on the ice. He was a team player in every game he played. What most people remember about Tim was his incredible strength. He did wrist curls with 150-pound weights, as if they were powder puffs. Horton seldom got into fights because he didn't want to hurt anyone. Other players knew better than to mess with him. If anybody was ever foolish enough, Tim would put a bear hug on him like a wrestler.

Tim was also known for walking through doors if he wanted to see you, especially after a night of beer drinking. When Tim came to your hotel door, you answered it! You might try to avoid others, but when you heard Tim giggling outside your room, you yelled out "Wait a minute! I'll be right there." If you didn't answer, he'd break the door down with his chest. Tim would pick up half the cost of a new door, but you had to pay for the rest. That's why Tim got prompt attention. Still, we all missed him when he was gone.

In 1970-71 we rebounded to fourth place in the East Division with 82 points. Playing on a line with Norm Ullman and Ron Ellis, I had my best year, with 30 goals and 30 assists. We started to click as a unit, and for the next two years we could compete with any line in the league. Ullman, Ellis, and I put up some good numbers, and we also prided ourselves on playing a two-way game. Two new goalies joined the Leafs, old pro Jacques Plante, and in a late-season trade with Philadelphia, Bernie Parent. If Plante was the great goalie in the sunset of his career, Parent was the new star on the horizon.

The Rangers beat us four games to two in the quarter-finals. What was maddening to me was that we should have won the series. We were up 2-1 in games but couldn't finish off New York when we had them on the ropes. For whatever reason, Plante had a terrible series, capped by Bob Nevin's overtime goal in the sixth game.

Another young man who joined our team in 1970 was Darryl Sittler, who proceeded to demonstrate that he was one of the most determined kids ever to lace on a pair of skates. Sittler worked relentlessly at every aspect of the game, and as he did, he became stronger, tougher, and more competent in shooting the puck.

Darryl and I hit it off immediately. We were both from small towns in Ontario, so we could relate to each other. We grew friendlier when we each bought homes close together in Mississauga. During the 1972 series against the Soviet Union, Darryl and his wife, Wendy, looked after our three daughters while Eleanor and I were in Moscow. Darryl and I also used to get into some great Ping-Pong games in my basement. These matches were almost as intense as a Stanley Cup playoff game! Darryl used this competitive spirit to make himself into a great hockey player, and he ended up being inducted into the Hall of Fame in 1989.

Bobby Baun rejoined the Leafs for the 1970-71 season. "Boomer" Baun knew just one style — straight ahead. He was as tough as nails, and even though he might lose a fight, he'd be right back in your face. Baun never took a step backwards and was noted for his bone-crunching bodychecks, not to mention his fearlessness when it came to blocking shots. You don't see too many guys like Bobby Baun around anymore.

I stayed pretty healthy during the 1971-72 season, playing in 73 games and scoring 38 times, a personal best. Still, we were unable to finish better than fourth place with 80 points, just four ahead of Detroit. Sometime in February 1972 King Clancy took over as coach of the team after Johnny McLellan got sick. King was one of the real characters in hockey. He had done it all in the NHL as a player, coach, referee, and now in management with the Leafs.

A fierce competitor in his playing days, he hadn't lost the desire to win. The trouble was, King coached as if he were still toiling in the 1930s. To a large extent the game had passed him by. Even so, he was good at keeping us loose and he had a heart as big as a house. We responded by going 9-3-3 during his brief stint behind the bench.

King was so funny to watch and listen to that we'd bite our fingers to stop laughing. One night we were playing Boston at home when Clancy saw Jim Dorey filing down the blade of his stick with a rasp. Jim was a defenceman who liked to wield a stick designed for goal scoring, which incensed King. Without thinking, Clancy grabbed the stick and whacked it over a garbage can, shattering it. "No wonder we can't play this game," he exploded. "We're using pansy hockey sticks!" This little tantrum had us in stitches, since King was always telling us, "You've got to lay the hickory on them." I guess he believed in the power of demonstration.

Once again we were eliminated by the Boston Bruins in the playoffs, this time in five games. The only highlight for us was Jim Harrison's overtime winner in the second game, a 4-3 victory in Boston. We kept it close, but the Bruins were too strong for us, what with superstars like Bobby Orr and Phil Esposito. They led the Bruins to a second Stanley Cup in three years.

I still thought our team wasn't in bad shape. We had some good forwards, a great goalie in Bernie Parent, and a young defence that was gaining in confidence and experience. Soon, though, I'd be playing with one of the greatest hockey teams ever assembled. The adventure of a lifetime was at hand.

3

The Battle Begins

"You're going where?" Alan Eagleson, my agent, demanded.

"The Rhine River," I replied. "In Germany. AP Parts, you know, the auto parts company I've been working for, they've set up a summer holiday package for Eleanor and me and 25 other couples."

"Cancel it. You're playing, and that's that," Eagleson barked, adjusting his glasses menacingly.

Alan Eagleson, as we all know now, played a key role in organizing Team Canada and the unprecedented eight-game battle it fought with the Soviet Union's National Team. The Eagle had a lot of faith in me, but in the spring of 1972 I wasn't convinced. Not about getting invited to the camp that would select the final team. I knew I had a pretty good shot at that. After all, in the 1971-72 season I'd scored a career high of 38 goals for the Leafs, which put me in the top ten that year. Thirty-five guys would be chosen to attend the camp in Toronto, and my pride and ego told me I just had to be one of them. No, my reservations had more to do with playing the Russians.

Like most Canadians, I was sick and tired of them beating our amateur teams. I really wanted to show them that we were the best. However, I also thought the NHL's elite would Zamboni the Soviets into the ice. It would be no contest, so why get excited? The Rhine River looked like more fun.

After I received my invitation to the Team Canada training camp, I still had some time to make my final decision. A meeting in Hay River, Alberta, helped me see the light. I was there with my Maple Leaf teammate Jim Harrison, Edmonton Eskimo football player Mike Law, and Canadian Olympic trapshooter Susan Nattrass. We were all there speaking at banquets. During our stay, we went fishing and, naturally, the discussion turned to the upcoming Canada-Russia hockey showdown. I told them about my Rhine River trip and how ambivalent I was about taking part in the series.

"You'd pass up a chance like that?" Susan Nattrass exclaimed, obviously perplexed. "You've got a tremendous opportunity to represent your country internationally. You've got to play. There may never be another series like it."

Susan was only an acquaintance, but given her status as a world-class athlete, I thought I should seriously consider her advice. Thanks to her, I now saw the hockey summit in a much bigger context. Eleanor was looking forward to going to Germany as much as I was. Both of us felt more involved since we had a large hand in organizing the entire event, but deep down we both knew I wanted to play in the series. Whatever the decision, I knew I'd have Eleanor's approval. She had always been supportive throughout my hockey career and she loved the game, so there was no real debate. We cancelled the Rhine trip, not fully aware we were about to embark on a great experience.

There were some players who turned down the invitation, but that didn't surprise me. Like me, they probably thought the effort wasn't worth giving up other commitments. The Russians would be pushovers. Where was the challenge? As for money, it was never a consideration when I made my decision. In fact, it was only much later that I realized we were going to be paid about $3,000, with a trip to Moscow thrown in for the wives.

Thanks to the NHL's battle with the World Hockey Association, some of our best players — Bobby Hull, J. C. Tremblay, Gerry Cheevers, and Derek Sanderson, to name a few — weren't allowed to play because they'd signed with the new league. Still, we looked as if we were going to be a formidable team. In goal we had Ken Dryden and Tony Esposito, the best two goalies in the NHL in 1972. Also available was solid veteran Eddie Johnston of the Boston Bruins. The goaltending looked strong and dependable.

A key to this series would be the defencemen. Their skating and puck-handling skills would be put to a real test, especially on the larger ice surface in Moscow. As one of the premier defencemen in the NHL, Brad Park was an obvious choice (24 goals and 73 points in 1971-72). A less obvious choice was Gary Bergman of Detroit, but he proved to be one of the real surprises and made an excellent partner for Park. The Chicago pair of Bill White and Pat Stapleton was a combination that inspired confidence. Guy Lapointe and Serge Savard, the Montreal Canadien duo, were the most talented. Rod Seiling of New York and Don Awrey of Boston were stay-at-home defencemen who could take care of their own end. Others included Jocelyn Guevremont and Dale Tallon of Vancouver and Brian Glennie of Toronto, none of whom played a game against the Russians.

We would, however, be missing the best defenceman in the game — Bobby Orr. Although he was at the training camp, his knee problems wouldn't allow him to play. There is no doubt we missed his talent for rushing the puck and controlling the power play. Orr was such a dominating player that he could change the outcome of this series all by himself. On the positive side Orr's absence would give others a chance to shine and grab the spotlight.

The forwards selected for this team were an impressive group with plenty of firepower. Phil Esposito was the dominating forward in the NHL (66 goals and 133 points in 1971-72). He controlled the slot area in front of the net as no other player could. Behind him at centre were great playmakers like Jean Ratelle, Stan Mikita, Red Berenson, Gilbert Perreault, and Marcel Dionne. Also included at centre was little-known Bobby Clarke. The group of wingers featured goal scorers like Frank Mahovlich (43 goals), Rod Gilbert (43 goals), Yvan Cournoyer (47 goals), Mickey Redmond (42 goals), and Rick Martin (44 goals). The grinders and corner men included people like J. P. Parise, Wayne Cashman, Bill Goldsworthy, Dennis Hull, Vic Hadfield, Peter Mahovlich, and Ron Ellis.

Naturally I was pleased that my Maple Leaf teammate and good friend Ron Ellis was invited to the camp. With the Leafs Ronnie and I played on the same line along with centre Norm Ullman. We hoped we'd be given a centre similar to Ullman at camp, but we figured we'd be relegated to a checking role on this strong team. Ellis was known as a top checker, and I was a good skater, so we could combine to force the play in the other teams end.

Despite the impressive competition that would be at the camp, I believed I belonged. I could skate with speed, which would be a big advantage in Moscow, had a hard shot, and could play a solid defensive game. Although I could force the play with my speed, I wasn't great at handling the puck. This didn't worry me, since there were many others on the team who could do this job effectively. I really believed that this competition with the greatest players in the NHL would bring out the best in me.

All of the players who were selected for the team certainly deserved to be there, but that didn't stop controversy from developing. First, there was the problem with the World Hockey Association players not being allowed to play because they had signed with the new league. From my point of view it was a case of the NHL playing politics. They were going to show their power by dictating who could play and who couldn't. The NHL wanted to bury the WHA and felt it wouldn't have been a smart move to give a rival league this type of exposure. While it would have been great to have Hull, Tremblay, and other guys available, there was nothing I or the other players could do about the situation. Besides, with the players that were selected we had more than enough talent and firepower to beat the Russians handily.

Second, there were a few surprises concerning who wasn't invited to camp. For example, Johnny Bucyk of Boston and Dave Keon of Toronto were excluded. I was surprised that Keon hadn't been asked since he was a great skater and checker, but the coaches were trying to build a team with various skills and not have too many of the same type of player. As we saw with the controversy over Steve Yzerman's exclusion from the 1991 Canada Cup team, difficult decisions have to be made when selecting an effective team for international competition.

Overall, I would say head coach Harry Sinden and his assistant John Ferguson did a great job in selecting a good mix of players. Sinden took a little heat for taking a Bobby Clarke ahead of a player like Dave Keon, but a

choice like that demonstrates why Sinden is still a top executive in the NHL. Sinden had also coached a Stanley Cup
winner with Boston in 1970. Ferguson was a very tough,
determined player in his day with five championship rings
to show for his career. I was really glad Ferguson was there
because he wasn't averse to telling someone what was on
his mind. There would be no messing around with Fergie
there. Basically I felt very comfortable with the coaches, and
they must have thought highly of my abilities since they selected me for the team. As the pressure mounted, Sinden
and Ferguson had to tell some NHL stars they weren't
going to play. That's not a job I would have wanted, but as
coaches they reacted extremely well and in retrospect they
made the correct choices.

Having made my decision to attend training camp, I
was quite anxious to get going. Not content to be merely
selected, I was keen on making the starting team!

Right from the beginning of camp on August 13 you
could see that some of the players had worked very hard
to get ready. It was just as obvious that others had done
very little in terms of preparation. Since I always kept
myself in good condition, I had a decided advantage over
those not in top shape.

Although we were never told anything, I assumed everybody would play at least two or three games. Some of
the better players might get into five or six games, but I
thought there would be no way anyone would play all
eight. For example, I was certain Ron Ellis, Brian Glennie,
and I would play the Toronto game and all the Montreal
Canadien players would be in the lineup for the first
game at the Forum. But that was only an assumption. As
the camp started up, competitiveness began to materialize
among the assembled players, a factor that can alter any
preconceived notions in a real hurry.

Prior to camp, Ron Ellis and I knew we would be linemates but speculated on who would be our centre. We figured we would be looked at as checkers because we were fast skaters and played an up-and-down game on the wings. As such, we hoped we'd get a player like Stan Mikita for our centre because his offensive skills might help us to be the fourth or fifth line at camp. About the last guy we wanted as a centreman was that diabetic kid from Philadelphia, Bobby Clarke.

Sure enough, at the first practice Bobby Clarke was our centre. Ellis and I both thought this assured us a checking role and would make us the last line at camp. We couldn't have been more wrong! The chemistry among the three of us developed immediately. Clarke was very serious and intense every time he stepped out on the ice. Some players just have that ability. He turned out to be tremendous and a real leader by example. I quickly got the feeling that Clarke would eat a skate blade if he had to — he was that dedicated to winning. He forechecked aggressively in the offensive end and worked hard at coming back defensively. Ellis and I were used to having Norm Ullman at centre when we played for the Leafs, and Clarke was a lot like Ullman, only younger and with a more abrasive style. Clarke's work ethic was contagious. The three of us sat down together early at camp and said, "Let's see if we can get into the first game," which wouldn't be easy, since we figured that a group of a dozen or so players had starting spots locked up and we weren't part of that elite. Being the underdogs made us all that more determined.

We were fortunate that our line stayed together all the time, while other players switched partners quite often. We were able to keep our unit intact by playing solid two-way hockey. We started to push one another and became more serious than most of the other players. Finally the extra work started to pay off, especially during the red/white intrasquad games, which were a real confidence builder for our line. We dominated the other lines, running them into the ice. Not only did we check, but we also scored. We had great confidence in one another, and everyone at camp knew we were playing well together and took notice.

For other players the combination never clicked, either because of a lack of seriousness or because the right chemistry never developed. You could see their frustration. For example, Gilbert Perreault and Rick Martin of Buffalo couldn't find a winger to work with them. Perhaps if NHL linemate Rene Robert had been there, it would have been different. On the other hand, the New York Rangers GAG (Goal-a-Game) line of Ratelle, Hadfield, and Gilbert couldn't get into gear as they had in the NHL. I know that if Ellis and I had been given another centre, things might not have worked so well for us, either. But our line meshed so effectively that there was no way the coaches could break it up.

On the whole, training camp was upbeat and positive. We played hard both on and off the ice. It was exciting to play with these players and a treat not having to play against them! I had an opportunity to appreciate their skills and a chance to share stories with these great athletes. As time went on, we became a close group.

But sometimes things got a little too casual, mainly as a result of our arrogance and cockiness. We simply had a hard time taking the opposition seriously. The coaches tried to warn us about the Russians, but we weren't really listening. Nobody knew much about the opposition, which meant we were dealing with the unknown. You tried to tell yourself that this was going to be tough.

However, your ego told you Canada had just too good a team.

In fact, we didn't just want to win; we wanted to humiliate the Russians. I thought it would be a tremendous embarrassment if we lost even one game! We wanted to beat them 10-0 and rub their noses in it but good. We knew we were the best. We knew that our system (i.e., democracy) was better than their system (i.e., communism). A 15-0 win in the first game would really show them.

Much has been made about the scouting report we received on the Russians, especially their goalie Vladislav Tretiak. We were told that Tretiak was generally weak with the glove, although, mind you, he had been scouted on the night before his marriage, not necessarily a good indication of his ability. But even if they had told us he was the greatest goalie in the game, our guys wouldn't have believed it. After all, who had he ever played against? I was sure Tretiak would be paralyzed when players such as Dennis Hull or Yvan Cournoyer fired a puck at him. He'd want to get out of Canada fast! The other Russians were only of average height and about 170 pounds, which meant we'd intimidate them by taking the body. Their eyes would be the size of saucers as we approached with a body check! Arrogance knew no bounds when it came to that first Team Canada.

If we as players had no apprehensions, then the coaches certainly did. Harry Sinden tried to get us motivated for the series by showing us films of the Whitby Dunlops, a team he captained to the world championships. The guys started to make jokes and said that Sinden looked like Charlie Chaplin as he skated around in the old black-and-white film. If a bunch of amateurs in crew cuts could beat the Russians, what would the finest

NHL players do to them? Since no one was taking this exercise very seriously, Sinden cut the session short.

But Sinden and Ferguson developed a solid five-point game plan: (1) apply offensive pressure; (2) play the NHL style; (3) shoot often from any angle; (4) be aggressive but deliver a hit only when in position to do so; and (5) no fighting. This was an excellent strategy, which would allow us to dictate the tempo of the game. How the Russians would adjust would determine how badly we beat them.

The media followed the camp closely, and the team generally received positive coverage, although I remember one Montreal newspaper writer, John Robertson, predicting that Canada would lose the series. I thought to myself, Who is this yahoo and what gives him the audacity to make such a prediction? I got to know John later and we became friends, but at the time I was very upset with him.

As the camp came to a close, the competition to get into the starting lineup really intensified. When the Russians arrived, we were able to see them practice, which only stoked the desire to represent Canada on the ice. The hype was really starting to build at this point, and I knew I had to get myself settled down. Our line had made the starting team, so it was now a matter of getting at the Russians and showing them who was superior.

It came as no surprise that Clarke, Ellis, and I would be in the starting lineup in Montreal on Saturday, September 2. Harry Sinden said we had been the best line at camp and deserved to start. We knew we were going to be counted on to check their top line and were confident we could score, as well. Ken Dryden was named as the starting goalie, and five defencemen — Bergman, Park, Lapointe, Awrey, and Seiling — were dressed for the game. Phil Esposito centred Yvan Cournoyer and Frank Mahovlich, the Rangers GAG line was intact for this game, and Peter Mahovlich, Mickey Redmond, and Red Berenson were also available. Obviously some players were disappointed that they weren't dressing, but since it was only the first game of the series, there would be plenty of time for everybody to see action. No one was too upset at this point.

The day of the game was fairly relaxed, but after getting to the Forum in the evening, the tension began to mount. It was fairly quiet in the dressing room at first, but then we really started to get pumped up. There was yelling and screaming about what we were going to do to the Soviets, and by the time we hit the ice, we were like caged animals suddenly released. In fact, we were probably too high. I know I had to calm myself down. Still, I was secure in the knowledge that with our game plan we were going to take it to them and intimidate the Russians rather easily.

After the opening ceremonies were concluded, the game started as if we had written the script. Phil Esposito swatted one into the Russian net after just 30 seconds of play. What a great feeling! The goal energized us even more, and you could feel the charge that went through the Forum crowd. On my first shift I took a tripping penalty with no harm done. Later, at 6:32 with a face-off in the Russian end, Clarke got the puck to Ellis off the draw. Then he gave it to me and I slapped it low along the ice just inside the post. I don't think Tretiak saw the shot that made it 2-0 for Canada. However, all was not well.

Actually I was concerned right after my first shift. Even though we were really throwing our weight around, you could see they weren't rattled. What unnerved me most was how cool they were, as if they were detached from the whole situation. They handled the puck with ease and skill and didn't show any sign of panic. The other noticeable feature was their conditioning, which was far superior to ours. On one shift I stayed out for forty seconds and returned to the bench, gasping for air. My Russian counterpart on that same shift wasn't even breathing hard! After scoring the goal, I sat next to Ellis and Clarke, and we all agreed that we were playing a great hockey team and that we were in for a long series.

It also proved to be a long night. The Russians tied the score 2-2 by the end of the first period, while in the next period our expectations really jumped off the track when Valeri Kharlamov scored two goals to give our opponents a 4-2 lead. On one goal Kharlamov whipped around defenceman Don Awrey to the outside, a move few could do in the NHL. Awrey pivoted to check Kharlamov, but the Russian skated past him, protecting the puck and then beating Dryden. Awrey couldn't lay a hand on him.

But we weren't about to admit defeat. At 8:22 of the third period Ellis and I set up Clarke for a goal to make it 4-3, which gave us a big lift. However, the Russians quickly dispelled any thoughts of a comeback by whipping in three goals for a 7-3 final.

The Russians weren't intimidated in any way, not physically or emotionally. They were obviously well trained. The fact that they were in our country playing in our arena didn't bother them at all. Their transition game was excellent, allowing them to capitalize on our turnovers with ease. When they had the puck, they were amazingly patient, passing it around in tic-tac-toe fashion. They were also effective in shooting the puck when you least expected a shot. We were more intense, but they were stronger physically and were rock-solid on their skates, which contributed to their success along the boards. There was much for us to be concerned about as we prepared for the next game.

Before preparing for the second game we had to deal with losing the series opener. It was a sickening feeling to say the least. My whole attitude about the Russians had changed. We were in for a dogfight, no question about it. I felt our line had played well, since we had scored two goals and only been on the ice for one of theirs after the issue had been decided. But there were changes that would have to be made. Our lack of conditioning in the stifling heat was painfully clear. Reinforcements would have to be brought in to rectify the situation. A new formula would have to be devised by Sinden and Ferguson.

The dressing room was quiet after the game, a marked contrast to the frenzy a few hours earlier. We didn't talk much, but we all had questions in our minds about what was going to happen next. Most of us tried to remain as calm and composed as Harry Sinden. "This is an eight-game series," he reminded us. "We lost the first game, but it's not the end of the world. Let's get a good night's sleep, and we'll get them in Toronto."

His words were reassuring, but I still had a sinking feeling. One thing we had to do for certain was get much better defensively. To help us do that we would never dress five defencemen again. It would take six to beat the Russians. With the speed of their transition game anyone who couldn't keep up with them would be left far behind. The right choices would have to be made, or we were going to get embarrassed again. Once more I was glad I wasn't in Harry Sinden's shoes.

Many Canadians felt a tremendous letdown after the first game. I make no apology for the way we played in the opener. Based on the information available, we had prepared as well as we could. Obviously the Russians were quite content to let us entertain whatever delusions we had about them. I felt that their system thrived to a large extent on deception and that the Russian players had to survive in a less than ideal situation. Their coaches were absolute dictators, and the players had no say in anything. However, we did have great respect for them as gifted athletes. One thing was certain: we weren't so cocky anymore. Harry Sinden and John Ferguson now had our complete attention.

I would have preferred more time off between games, but we had only one day to prepare for the second game two days later in Toronto. The coaches added Wayne Cashman, J. P. Parise, Bill Goldsworthy, Stan Mikita, and Serge Savard to the lineup, while Dryden was replaced with Tony Esposito.

These moves were very necessary to give our team a different look. I was especially glad to see Serge Savard added, even though he hadn't had a great camp. Savard was a take-charge defenceman who was extremely effective under pressure. Some of the new forwards, like Cashman and Parise, were consistent grinders who could slow down the Russians and perhaps intimidate them just a little. We knew we couldn't let them freewheel, because if we did, their superior conditioning would allow them to run right over us. We had to shut them down and outplay them defensively. There was no way we could afford to lose two in a row.

As a Maple Leaf, I was familiar with the almost reserved nature of Toronto crowds. But on this night the atmosphere crackled with anticipation. My mother and family were in attendance, and since this was the only game in Toronto, I really wanted to show my stuff. Emotions in the rink, on our bench, and on the ice were at a fever pitch.

Even though we outplayed the Russians in the first period, we couldn't score. But neither did they. Despite our frustration, we played a patient game. Then, finally, at 7:14 of the second period Phil Esposito scored a goal from the slot as a delayed penalty was being called on the Russians. Espo took a stick right across the back but still managed to control the puck and fire it home, much to our jubilation.

At 1:19 of the third period Yvan Cournoyer took a pass from Brad Park at the Russian blue line along the boards. He blew past the defenceman and went in to beat Tretiak, scoring the type of goal characteristic of the man they called the Roadrunner. Now we were up 2-0 and apparently on the right track. Or were we? Four minutes or so later Alexander Yakushev, an impressive Russian winger, skipped a rebound past Tony Esposito, making it 2-1. Then, as if we didn't have enough problems, Pat Stapleton took a penalty.

Potential disaster was averted by Peter Mahovlich. He and Phil Esposito were out killing the penalty when Espo was able to spring Mahovlich free with a pass. Peter made a great move on the lone Russian defenceman and stuffed it behind Tretiak, recording one of the most beautiful and dramatic goals anyone had ever seen. The Toronto crowd went crazy, and we all jumped off the bench to congratulate Peter. Now we were on track again, and Frank Mahovlich's goal, making it 4-1, was the icing on the cake.

The team was ecstatic in the dressing room after the game. The universe was unfolding as it should. Unfortunately our cocky arrogance reared its ugly head again, but we would pay dearly for our rediscovered superiority, starting with the next game.

We caught the Russians a little flat-footed in Winnipeg on September 6, and J. P. Parise scored the opener less than two minutes into the first period. Parise was a good role player who never failed to barrel into the corners and work frantically to dig out the puck. But before we could get too comfortable Vladimir Petrov scored a short-handed goal, which was answered by Jean Ratelle, who put us back up 2-1.

Phil Esposito gave us a two-goal cushion at 4:19 of the second period assisted by Cashman and Parise. But the speedy Kharlamov zipped in to bag another shorthanded goal, making it 3-2. Kharlamov wasn't only fast; he had excellent moves and could fire a puck with pinpoint accuracy. Grim and determined, I used my speed to chase a pass from Bobby Clarke over the Russian blue line. The puck took an odd bounce, enabling me to beat the defenceman to it and fire it from the hash mark of the face-off circle. My shot sailed low to Tretiak's stick side, beating him and putting us up by two goals once more. As if on cue, though, the Soviets responded with two late goals to make it 4-4 before the second period was over.

In the final period there was no scoring and we were quite lucky to hold on to a tie with a team that clearly outplayed us. There was no doubt we'd let this game slip away, twice losing two-goal leads. The atmosphere in the dressing room was one of confused unhappiness.

Tretiak's play made it abundantly clear that we had some tough slogging ahead. He was very cool with no glaring weaknesses and stopped just about everything we fired at him. In the Winnipeg game I had a great chance when I found myself in the slot. I onetimed a pass that I was sure was heading for the back of the net. I even started to raise my hands, but Tretiak stopped the shot. I was so impressed by the save that I skated over and tapped him on the pads. He just nodded back.

The series was starting to resemble a roller coaster ride. A win in Vancouver would put us back on top in this series, so we were looking forward to our trip to the West Coast, despite the letdown over the tie.

There were some surprising lineup changes for the game in Vancouver on September 8. Goalie Tony Esposito, who was playing some great hockey, was dropped for Ken Dryden. Also deleted were Ratelle, Mikita, Parise, Cashman, Peter Mahovlich, Lapointe, and Savard. Added to the team were Rod Gilbert, Bill Goldsworthy, Dennis Hull, Vic Hadfield, Rod Seiling, Don Awrey, and Gilbert Perreault. The coaches were under a certain amount of pressure to play everyone. Players who had given up their summer to participate wouldn't be very happy watching from the bench. Besides, we hadn't finished well in Winnipeg, so maybe a shake-up was needed.

But all of the juggling turned out to be for nothing. We started the Vancouver game poorly, and the Russians stung us for two quick goals. Bill Goldsworthy, who was told to play it tough, had drawn penalties for cross-checking and elbowing. Naturally, the Russians took advantage and scored two power play goals. In the second period Perreault scored a nice goal on an individual effort, but the Soviets added two more to make it 4-1. Goldsworthy atoned for his sins somewhat by bringing us closer with a goal at 6:54 of the third, but Vladimir Shadrin made it a three-goal lead at 11:05. Then Dennis Hull added a late goal with less than a minute to play, making the final score a more respectable 5-3.

More than anything this game will be remembered as the one where Team Canada got booed on home ice.

Make no mistake, we were bad. No matter what we tried, it didn't work. I know I didn't feel good on the ice at all. I couldn't seem to find my legs during the entire game. But when Frank Mahovlich was loudly booed for sitting on Tretiak, I thought to myself, What am I doing here? I was starting to feel sorry for myself. After all, I'd given up my summer to play for Canada, and now the crowd was cheering the enemy and booing us!

In the dressing room between the second and third periods Phil Esposito and I talked about the situation. We dressed next to each other, and I turned and asked Phil, "Why are these people booing us? Can't they see we're trying? Our own people are turning on us."

"It's not right," Phil agreed. "What do these people want from us? We're playing for Canada. Don't they realize that?"

The situation required leadership and that's exactly what Phil Esposito provided in a postgame television interview with Johnny Esaw on the CTV national network. In part he said, "To the people of Canada, I say we tried. We did our best. We're really disheartened, disappointed, and disillusioned. We can't believe we're getting booed in our own building. I'm really, really disappointed. I can't believe it. Some of our guys are really down in the dumps. They have a good team. Let's face facts. We came because we love Canada. I don't think it's fair that we should be booed."

When he returned to the dressing room, he told me what he had done and said, "I told them!" I wasn't surprised. Phil is a very expressive person who isn't afraid to speak publicly. I think our talk between periods helped him sort out what he was going to say. Phil was also careful to mention that he wasn't speaking about all Canadians. He added he would come back and apologize if the

Russian people did the same to their team. As captain, Phil did his job beautifully. Our team was completely behind him and supported his sentiments. We were getting crucified from all angles and needed someone to speak out for us. Phil's words not only lifted our spirits but seemed to inspire a change in attitude among Canadians in general.

As soon as Espo returned to the dressing room, he got a phone call from a woman in Newfoundland. She called Phil to tell him he was dead on with his speech. People across Canada started to react just as we had hoped. They supported us with cards, letters, petitions, telegrams, and all kinds of messages, wishing us luck and setting the stage for the nearly 3,000 people who made the trip to Moscow with us. Canadians had been shocked by the outcome so far, but they responded with the boost we would need on our opponent's home turf.

However, no matter what was said the situation was still pretty dismal. We had been pretty certain we'd have a commanding lead in the series by now. Instead we had dug a hole that looked almost bottomless. As we left the Pacific Coliseum, we all knew the fun had vanished from the series. All-out war stared us in the face. It was time to see how much grit and determination we had.

4

Shoot-out in Moscow

"You've got to let me play!" I insisted.

Harry Sinden looked at me, concern written in his face. "That was a pretty bad spill you took, Paul."

"You've got a concussion, son," the team doctor warned. "I can't let you go out there again."

"Coach?" I asked, staring at Sinden.

"Go!"

I'd been tripped while skating at full speed and slammed into the end boards, hitting my head and knocking myself out cold. Thank goodness I was wearing a helmet or I might have been killed! We were in the second period of that first game in Moscow's Luzhniki Arena, and there was no way I was going to miss out on the action. They'd have had to carry me out in a pine box.

The road to Moscow had been a long one in a series that was supposed to be a lark. On Saturday, September 16, we played the first of two exhibition games against the Swedish National Team in Stockholm. The games were a good idea, since they gave us the chance to get used to the larger European ice surface. It also gave us the opportunity to experience European refereeing first-hand. That experience wasn't pleasant.

I played in the opening game against the Swedes and

scored a goal and added one assist in a 4-1 victory. Our line continued its good play, and the bigger ice surface helped us to read plays better and maintain a solid two-way game. We were still the best line on the team.

The Swedes weren't nearly as aggressive as the Russians. They preferred to play a more controlled type of game. Certainly they weren't prepared for the confrontational style our team utilized. Our guys were gearing up to play the Russians and letting out a certain amount of frustration when we played the Swedes. As a result, these two games turned out to be ugly affairs.

The second contest ended in a 4-4 tie and resembled a battlefield more than a hockey game. We hammered the Swedes relentlessly. They didn't respond directly. Instead, they butt-ended and speared us every chance they got. Interference seemed to be their sole game strategy. Of course, we retaliated. They counted on that, and consequently we ended up in the penalty box. Wayne Cashman nearly had his tongue ripped out of his mouth by Ulf Sterner, while Swedish defenceman Lars-Eric Sjoberg had his nose broken. Naturally the Swedish press splashed Sjoberg's battered mug all over the place.

Two good things came out of our games with the Swedes. First, we started to come together as a team. We realized that the fun and games were over and that we had to prepare much more seriously for the Russians. We were all business now. Second, judging by the inferior refereeing in Europe, we could expect to be penalized repeatedly if we continued to play the NHL style of game. If we wanted to beat the Soviets, adjustments would have to be made.

We arrived in Moscow on Tuesday, September 20, and it didn't take long for things to go sour. Three players — Vic Hadfield, Rick Martin, and Jocelyn Guevremont —

decided to leave the team and return to Canada. Martin and Guevremont hadn't played against the Russians, while Hadfield had been used sparingly in just two games. I think they knew they weren't going to see any action in Moscow and I felt badly for them. Their frustration at the team's performance and their relegation to the bench must have been unbearable. I know I was grateful to be playing. Anything else would have been sheer torture.

Still, although, Hadfield and Martin were two of the top wingers in the NHL, neither of them deserved to play. I know if I had been the coach, I wouldn't have played them. That doesn't mean I had any animosity towards these players. I don't think the other players did, either. When the "me" became greater than the "we," it was time to leave. The same could be said about centre Gilbert Perreault's departure a few days later. We didn't need any further distractions at this point. With the benefit of hindsight some or all of the four who left might have done things differently, but pride can be a brutal thing to deal with, especially in certain circumstances. I certainly didn't judge them, because if I had been in their position, I might have left, too.

On the other side of the coin, there were players who weren't going to play much or at all but who refused to reverse their commitment to the team. Brian Glennie, Eddie Johnston, Mickey Redmond, Dale Tallon, and Marcel Dionne all made valuable contributions. They cheered us on and were a positive influence on the team, even though they knew they weren't going to get into the series against the Russians.

The team started to come together by putting personal issues aside and working in unison. We had a lot of big egos on the team and each player had different talents. Some of the players were great rivals in the NHL, but once we started playing, we put the team first. I'm not saying all the guys socialized with each other off the ice, but we were true professionals when it came to getting the job done. And what a job it was!

Although there were four games to play in the series, the coaches insisted we concentrate on one game at a time. This was a good way to get us focused, and we knew a win would restore our badly sagging confidence. Harry Sinden was one of the coolest, most composed coaches in the business. Whenever he was on the bench he was in total control. We came to understand the opposition better as we gained more information about them, and Sinden was invaluable on this score, if we would only listen.

Harry's assistant, John Ferguson, was the more excitable of the two. Sometimes John looked as intense as when he played with the Montreal Canadiens. He'd get that rage in his eyes and blow his cool, but he kept us loose and motivated. All and all, Fergie and Harry made a great pair.

On Friday, September 22, when we finally resumed the series with the Soviets, Luzhniki Arena was a circus, not because of the grim Russians in attendance, but because of the 3,000 frenzied Canadian fans who had come to cheer us on. I don't think the Soviets there, including Leonid Brezhnev and Alexei Kosygin, had ever seen or heard anything like it — hockey mania NHL-style, complete with bugles, chants, and raucous flag waving.

The party atmosphere was only amplified when Phil Esposito tripped on a flower and landed on his rear end during the pregame introductions. Phil got to his feet quickly and hammed it up for the delirious crowd, which only added fuel to their already raging hilarity. We couldn't have asked for a better tension reliever. Still, when I think back about Phil's pratfall, I wonder if it was a harbinger for what was to come.

But who could think about premonitions, bad or good, in the first two periods of that game. We opened the scoring late in the first when J. P. Parise knocked in a nice pass from Gilbert Perreault, who was playing his last game. Early in the second period I gave Bobby Clarke a pass just off a face-off in the Russian end. Clarke bulled his way in front of Tretiak and stuffed the puck between the Russian's pads. Then I scored at 11:58 from Guy Lapointe and Clarke to make it 3-0. What a start!

Later, in the second period, I took my somersault into the end boards and was knocked out. But soon I was back in the thick of things, doctor's advice notwithstanding. The shutout came to an abrupt end when the Russians made it 3-1 at 3:34 of the third period, but a little over a minute later I took a great pass from Clarke and broke in alone on Tretiak. He backed in and I slapped it through his pads to make it 4-1 with about 15 minutes to play.

But our lead didn't last long. The roof caved in on us when the Soviets netted two goals in eight seconds. The first by Viacheslav Anisin was a beautiful tip-in off a shot from the point. The tip-in was something the Russians were especially adept at, since they were fond of leaving a man at the edge of the crease to redirect a shot or pass. It was a play we could never defend against in a short-handed situation.

Yet another tip-in tied the score at 11:41, and they scored the winner at 14:46 as Vladimir Vikolov stole the puck at our blue line and broke in to beat Tony Esposito, who slammed his stick on the ice in disgust. Final score: 5-4.

The unthinkable had happened. We had lost again.

What had gone wrong? Obviously we had reverted to typical NHL thinking. Buoyed by a commanding lead, we had coasted and lost our concentration, which was certain suicide when playing against the Soviets. They were quick to pounce on turnovers and get their transition game going so fast that before you knew what had hit you, the puck was in the net.

There were a couple of positive notes to come from this game. First, the nearly 3,000 Canadian fans in the arena were a tremendous lift for the team. When we came out onto the ice, they'd drown out the Russian fans and go crazy. Not only did that perk up our guys, I think it also affected the Russians. After all, they had heard us booed at home. Now in their own rink these lunatic Canadians were cheering us on like nothing else I've ever seen. They had to wonder what was going on. Many of the Canadian fans stayed at our hotel in Moscow, and it was great to have them with us, since we thought we'd been abandoned back home. Second, even with the loss we had played better as a team and, more important, our physical conditioning was improving with each game. Although we had a lapse in the third period, we had definitely gained confidence.

The dressing room was sombre after the game, but we realized that we hadn't lost the series yet. Winners learn from their mistakes. We knew we had to win three in a row in their own backyard to take the series, but somehow we still thought we could.

One person who never doubted we would win was Alan Eagleson, who was a tremendous help to the coaches and players, often acting as a buffer. He had to handle many issues on behalf of the players. For example, we learned in Europe that the Russians were going to put the wives in a separate hotel. We told Al flat out that we wouldn't go unless the wives were allowed to stay with us. He took care of the situation.

Al dealt with all the administrative issues, such as who was to referee, when we would practise, and so on. He handled the Russian officials in his own inimitable way, steamrolling over people on both sides if he had to. But he got things done. Over in Moscow the Russians held all the cards. They knew, however, they would have Al to contend with, and we were lucky to have him on our side.

One thing you quickly learn about Eagleson is that he's a determined competitor. He'll do whatever it takes to win. If I went to war with anybody, I'd want Al on my side. He was never negative and never lost confidence in our team, even during the darkest moments. He never wavered because he believed we would find a way to win. Whenever he spoke to the team he gave us motivation. No doubt about it, the Eagle had a Canadian maple leaf tattooed on his chest.

With Al and his staff looking after all the behind-the-scenes dealings, I tried not to let any distractions affect me throughout the series. I knew my line was going to play, which allowed me to focus strictly on hockey. I was a role player in this series, not a superstar. I did more listening than talking. Following the game plan was all I was concerned with. I had a job to do.

As far as the team went, the leadership role fell to Phil Esposito, mostly because of what he did on the ice. Phil did everything for the team. He took a regular turn, played the power play, killed penalties, double-shifted, you name it. His stamina was amazing. If Bobby Orr was the best defenceman in all of hockey, Espo was without doubt the top forward. He was like a polar bear in the slot. Even the Russians started to call him "the man with the big heart." He wouldn't quit. He just kept coming back for more. Phil worked as hard as anyone I've ever seen. He won a couple of Stanley Cups with the Bruins, but this series would be the highlight of his career.

We made a few changes for game six on September 24, adding Serge Savard, Dennis Hull, Red Berenson, and Ken Dryden. Rod Seiling, Frank Mahovlich, and Tony Esposito sat this one out. I remember trying to pump up Dennis Hull for this game by calling him Moses. He was going to lead us out of the wilderness. As for Savard, I always felt better with him behind the blue line. I knew he'd get us out of trouble quickly.

After no scoring in the first period, the Russians got the first goal at 1:12 of the second for a 1-0 lead. But Moses, I mean Dennis Hull, tied it for us at 5:13, putting in Rod Gilbert's rebound. Yvan Cournoyer scored at 6:21 off a pass from Red Berenson, and seconds later I intercepted a pass in the centre ice area, took a couple of strikes over the Russian blue line, and fired a low shot that went in just inside the post past a screened Tretiak, making it 3-1. Then Yakushev added a goal for the Soviets, and the score was 3-2 at the end of the second.

There was no scoring in the final period and we checked them effectively. We were outshot 17-7 in the third, but Dryden enjoyed his best game of the series. We even managed to kill a late penalty given to Ron Ellis.

Victory was sweet, I can tell you. All those crazy Canadian fans went wild and, seeing that, I knew why we were there. I could feel the confidence building again.

If we were going to win the series, though, we would somehow have to find a way to deal with the officiating. The international hockey rules called for a system of two referees and no designated linesmen. That setup proved to be worse than we anticipated, especially in Europe, where the referees were very poor skaters and generally incompetent in calling the games. Joseph Kompalla, a West German, was particularly bad and certainly biased in his calls. The coaches tried their best to make the officials aware of their concern, and as a player, I had to realize I had no control over the situation. However, when any of us were on the ice, it wasn't always easy to maintain our cool, largely because we weren't used to this type of officiating.

To the European officials the Canada-Soviet series was just another string of games. There was nothing special about them. And even if Kompalla was a West German, he was still a European. We were North Americans, and his sympathies were obvious, Communist government notwithstanding. The Russians had a lot of influence in international hockey, and a European referee would be unwilling to incur their displeasure.

Even without the politics, we realized European referees called a much different game than their NHL counterparts. We weren't getting away with the kind of stuff our own referees ignored all the time. Many people were critical of the Russians for their dirty play, but the reality was that they were just hitting us back. For every shot they gave us, we probably gave them two or three. More than a few times we literally assaulted them, and they had no intention of taking it on the chin.

Our team certainly had players who normally played a physical game. Bobby Clarke was one of those players, and he took it upon himself to whack Valeri Kharlamov's ankle with a two-handed slash. Kharlamov was hobbled considerably after the sixth game, which was obviously to our advantage. I don't recall Clarke saying that he planned to whack Kharlamov; he just went out and did it. But that's the Canadian style of play — tough, aggres-

sive, and emotional. We had to face facts. The only way
we were going to win was to slow the Russians down by
playing in the style we knew best. So we received a lot of
penalties, but we got away with a great deal, as well.
Under the circumstances, I don't apologize for the way
we played. However, upon reflection I would have liked
to have seen a higher level of sportsmanship.

I found it quite easy to get all worked up and take out
my frustrations on the ice because I hated the Russians
and their system. Their way of doing things was very ma-
nipulative, working everything to their advantage. There
was psychological warfare going on in a whole variety of
areas, which aggravated us the whole time we were in
the Soviet Union. Nothing ever seemed to be organized.

Once, we were scheduled for a 10:00 a.m. practice at
Luzhniki Arena but couldn't get on the ice because a
group of kids were occupying it and wouldn't leave. In
Canada this type of thing would never happen at the professional level. So we had to resort to firing a few pucks
at the kids, who were gathered at the other end of the
rink. Only then did we get our ice.

In the afternoons I usually napped but could never settle down for a good sleep. The phone would ring with no
one on the other end. This happened to a lot of us. I suppose all of these hang-ups could have been a coincidence,
considering how poorly trained their people were, but at
the time I wasn't about to believe anything like that. I
was sure this was just another Russian ploy to disrupt
our game.

As if things like that weren't enough, the struggle for
food made life a real adventure. Even though we'd
brought over enough steaks for the players and the
wives, they quickly disappeared. The Russian cooks sold
the steaks to others in search of a decent meal, many of

whom turned out to be our zany Canadian fans. For about ten dollars U.S. you could get just about anything you wanted, including those precious steaks! The only two Russian dishes that were acceptable to me were borscht and chicken Kiev. The rest was just terrible. To irritate us more, our beer was hijacked, too!

The search for an acceptable meal took a funny twist one night thanks to Bill White and Pat Stapleton. The two Blackhawk defencemen started a story about a Chinese restaurant they'd found that had great food. They told people to meet in the lobby where buses would take them to the restaurant and a night out. The Chicago duo managed to convince quite a few people, including someone who cancelled the meal to be served at the hotel. When people finally realized that it was all a practical joke, they started to wonder how they could have been such idiots to believe such a story. It shows how desperate we all were for a good meal.

I think I was probably luckier than most because Eleanor had anticipated our food problems and brought over a suitcase full of items such as peanut butter, chocolate bars, granola, and cookies. When the other players found out about our stash, they came to our door, looking for goodies. My wife was also able to correct a problem with our hotel room. Most rooms in the hotel featured separate beds, which couldn't be put together because of the size of the room. Luckily Eleanor arrived early and got the authorities to give us a room big enough to shove the twin beds together. Otherwise I might not have survived.

Eleanor is a smart, intuitive individual who can read me like a book. She has always been good at finding ways to help and contribute. Having her there in Russia was certainly a very steadying factor in helping me to stay on track. She never let me get too far over the edge.

Considering some of the things we observed and endured in Russia it's surprising we didn't explode. For one thing there was no privacy. Each time you left your room your key had to be handed over to the warden of the floor, who was there at all times. Talk about prison! To add insult to injury, we were pretty certain the Russians had bugged the entire place. We had no proof, of course, but even if the rooms were bugged, it didn't bother me. I never let things like that interfere with what I wanted to do. Other players started talking to mirrors, light fixtures, and bureaus, saying things like, "You Commie so-and-so." Naturally the stories have grown wilder and wilder over the years.

The way the Russians treated their own people was really unbelievable. We would throw gum and candies to kids during a workout or pregame warm-up only to see Red Army soldiers step on the kids' fingers and take the sweets away. I thought to myself, How can they do something like that? Another time we went as a group to the Tretyakov Art Gallery. When we got there, the soldier at the door put his rifle in front of the people waiting to get in and pushed them back so that we could get through. Needless to say, there was no resistance or questioning. Things like that would happen in the course of a game, as well. On one occasion Alexander Maltsev returned to the bench and a doctor injected a hypodermic into his foot right through the sock. It made me cringe.

Even if the system of government was rotten, we soon realized that the average Russian was no different than his Canadian counterpart. They were just trying to make a living like the folks back home. The Russian hockey players were essentially a decent group of people trying to survive in a brutal system. Make no mistake, there were things to admire about Russia. They had beautiful museums, the very talented Bolshoi ballet, the breathtaking Moscow Circus, but in 1972 I really didn't enjoy these excursions because I was so focused on hockey. Still, I left Russia feeling very lucky and appreciative of the life I had in Canada.

We only had a couple of changes for the seventh game on Tuesday, September 26. Bill Goldsworthy and Tony Esposito were added, while Ken Dryden and Red Berenson sat out. Ron Ellis and I started to see action on the power play, which paid off early in the first period when we combined with Phil Esposito to make it 1-0. I passed the puck to Ellis in the corner, he threw it to Phil right in front of the crease, and Espo beat Tretiak for a goal that wasn't an official power play effort.

Yakushev broke in over the blue line and slapped a bullet through Tony Esposito's pads to tie the score. Then Vladimir Petrov deked Esposito to make it 2-1 for them. Before the end of the first period Serge Savard pulled one of his patented "spinaramas" at the Russian blue line and passed to Phil Esposito in the slot, who beat Tretiak with a low, hard shot to tie the score 2-2. Phil was so big and strong that the Russians couldn't handle him. When they did knock him down, he quickly got up and banged away at the puck.

There was no scoring in the second period, but early in the third we made it 3-2 on a goal by Rod Gilbert, who took a puck off the end boards and beat Tretiak with a nice backhand shot. However, we took a penalty, and Yakushev tipped one in just off the edge of the crease for a typical, virtually unstoppable Russian power play goal. Rangy, with good moves and excellent hands, Yakushev was a great hockey player and could take advantage of just about any opportunity.

A tie game was no good for us. Victory was the only

thing we would settle for. As the clock ticked away, I thought we should pull our goalie. We had to do something to win this game. Then, with about three minutes to play and the teams playing four skaters a side, I got on for what was likely my final shift of the game. Somehow I knew I was going to score.

Savard hit me with a pass in the centre ice area. Quickly I shifted to beat one of the forwards who was backchecking. Then, on my own at their blue line, I barrelled in on the two defencemen. The one on my left made a move to swipe at the puck with his stick just as I was trying to put it between his legs. He took himself out of the play by looking at the puck, which ended up bouncing off the inside of his skate. With a little luck I was able to pick up the puck again and start toward the net. By this time the other defenceman came across to take me out. He actually tripped me, but fortunately I had the puck in front and managed to keep my stick clear. As I fell, Tretiak started to drop to his knees, hoping to block a low shot. That left me no choice but to try to drill the puck high. With Tretiak down I had just enough room to put my shot over his shoulder, just under the crossbar, for the winning goal.

Not only was this one of the greatest thrills of my career, it was easily the best goal I ever scored in my life. I normally beat people with my speed; stick-handling was never my forte. I was fortunate to get the right bounce, but there is no doubt that this was the best individual effort I ever made. When you're totally focused, you can sometimes do things you never dreamed possible.

The guys jumped off the bench and knocked me down during a wild celebration behind the Russian net. Then we killed off the final two minutes of the third period to win 4-3 and tie the series. If we hadn't won the game, the final contest would have been meaningless.

Although we had another game to go, I thought I'd reached the peak of my athletic career. There was no way things could get any better. Knowing I was playing very well and scoring two-game winning goals gave me great satisfaction, but our task as a team wasn't complete. We had to go to the well one more time.

After the seventh game was over, I put my arm around Ron Ellis in the dressing room and said, "Chevy, you're going to get the winning goal in the final game." We called Ellis "Chevy" for short because he looked like Canadian boxer George Chuvalo.

"Sure," Ronnie replied, laughing, but he knew I meant it.

Ronnie wasn't only my Leaf teammate but a very good friend. He hadn't scored a goal all series long, but we would never have been in a position to win if not for players like him. After the first game, Ronnie was given the assignment to check Kharlamov, and he did a masterful job. It wasn't an easy task, but he accepted it willingly because he was a dedicated team player. Ronnie worked in the trenches and did what was required of him. You don't win without people like Ron Ellis.

If there is one enduring picture I have of Ronnie in this series, it was late in the sixth game. We were up 3-2 and needed the win to keep our hopes alive in the series. A borderline call by the referee gave Ronnie a holding penalty with only 2:21 to play in the third. He sat in the penalty box, pounding his fist on his thigh. It must have been the longest two minutes of his life. I think I said a prayer for him, because I knew that if the Russians somehow scored, Ronnie would blame himself. He was the kind of guy who would do a great job but would always remember his one mistake. On the other hand, I was the exact opposite. If I did anything right, I'd be happy about it. Our different personalities seemed to balance our friendship. As it turned out, we killed the penalty and won the game.

At the beginning of the series I never imagined that it would come down to one game. I also never thought that we'd have to battle back as we had just to tie the series. Now, on Thursday, September 28, we had a chance to complete a fantastic comeback. There was no doubt that this was bigger than winning the Stanley Cup. Twice I had played in the Cup finals with the Detroit Red Wings, losing on both occasions, and I'll never forget that bottomless, sick feeling that made me cry. This time I was determined there would be no more tears. I had a once-in-a-lifetime opportunity to be a part of something everyone would remember. I just hoped I could control my emotional level, as did the rest of the team.

Unfortunately we got into trouble early. Bill White and Peter Mahovlich received holding penalties, putting us down two men. Not surprisingly, Yakushev put in a rebound at the edge of our goal crease. But on our own power play we caught a break when a Russian defenceman knocked in Brad Park's rebound past Tretiak to tie it 1-1. Phil Esposito, who had tried to bang the puck in, got credit for the goal but never really touched it.

At this point J. P. Parise got a minor penalty for interference. The call wasn't made by the official closest to the play, but by our West German friend Kompalla, who was on the other side of the ice. The penalty incensed Parise, and he swung his stick at the German as if he were going to strike him. Naturally he was thrown out of the game, which really upset our players and coaches.

When J. P. got tossed, I was ready to leave. "Let's get out of here," I said to Ron Ellis. If Harry Sinden had given us the order, I would have been out of there in a flash. It was so frustrating to watch these officials make a mockery of the game, but we had come too far to quit now.

On yet another power play the Russians scored a goal on a low shot from the point, beating a screened Ken Dryden. Then Jean Ratelle and Brad Park combined on a neat passing play to tie it at 2-2. A couple of Russians collided at their own blue line, allowing Park to come in to take a pass from Ratelle, which he whipped past Tretiak.

Just 21 seconds into the second period the Russians got a break when Vladimir Shadrin put in a puck that bounced off the wire fence behind our goal and landed right on his stick in front of the net. Dryden tried to catch the carom off the fence but missed, as did our defence-man, who took a swipe at the puck. At 10:32, though, Bill White jumped into the play to knock in a perfect pass from Rod Gilbert, tying the game at 3-3.

Off a face-off in our end, Espo let the Russians' centre go for just a split second, which was all he needed to tap the puck to Yakushev, who was right in front of our net and able to beat Dryden at 11:43. Shadrin scored another power play goal for them at 16:44, putting us down 5-3 at the end of two periods.

Between periods we agreed we couldn't open up the play too much to get back into the game. Still, we had to get one early to build momentum and keep things close. The strategy worked. Peter Mahovlich did some excellent work along the boards, then flipped a pass to Esposito. Phil knocked the pass down in front of the net, and on his second swing surprised Tretiak to make it 5-4. At this stage our confidence was sailing. We had fought with the referees, killed off penalties, survived some bad breaks, but we were still alive. And the Russians helped us by becoming defensive.

At 12:56 we tied the game when Yvan Cournoyer swatted in Espo's rebound. Phil did all the work on this goal, bulling his way down the wing, fighting off three Russians, and taking the shot that Cournoyer backhanded over a sprawled Tretiak. At this point we had to rescue Alan Eagleson from the clutches of Russian soldiers. He was quite upset when the red light didn't go on for Cournoyer's goal. We took him over to our bench for safekeeping, but this whole situation was just another part of the off-ice circus that surrounded the series.

A 5-5 tie wouldn't have been a bad ending to the series, but no one on our team was prepared to settle for that. We had to find a way to win, and there was no overtime!

As we got into the last minute of play, I stood up at our bench and yelled three times at Peter Mahovlich to come off so I could get on the ice. It wasn't our line's turn, but I honestly felt I could get a goal. I can't explain why, but I just had this feeling, just as I'd had in the previous game. For whatever reason, Peter came to the bench and I catapulted myself over the boards to join the play in the Russian end. As I got on, the puck went to Cournoyer on the far boards. I screamed at him for a pass that I hoped to one-time at the net because I had a clear shot, but I had to reach back for the puck with all my momentum pushing me forward. I missed and their defenceman neatly tripped me, causing me to fall and slide into the boards behind their net. Immediately I thought, Get up. Get the puck and come back down to try to score.

The Russians, with a great chance to clear the zone, failed to control the puck, allowing the relentless Phil Esposito to whack the loose disk towards the goal. Tretiak stopped Phil's shot but couldn't smother it. By this time I was standing alone in front of Tretiak to pick up the rebound. I tried to slide a shot along the ice, but Tretiak got a piece of it. The puck came right back to me, and with Tretiak down I slid it along the ice for the winning goal. There were only 34 seconds left to play!

It all happened so fast, but I can recall a couple of emotions quite clearly. Just as the puck was going in, I thought, Dad would have loved to have seen this. My father was perhaps the most influential person in my being a professional hockey player, and it was sad knowing that we couldn't share this incredible moment. The brief feeling of melancholy quickly turned into jubilation as I thought, We've done it! I jumped into Cournoyer's arms, and all the guys flung themselves off the bench and raced towards us. The impossible had happened!

I skated back to the bench and told Sinden, "Harry, I'm done." I knew I couldn't play those last 34 seconds. I was physically and emotionally drained. In any event, we held them off to win 6-5 and take the series four wins to three with one game tied.

After the game was over, I was interviewed on television, so I didn't get into the dressing room for a few minutes. When I walked in, everybody cheered. I sat in the dressing room for about 45 minutes before I even began to take off my equipment. I was totally exhausted. There was a real sense of satisfaction in the room. It had been a tremendous struggle, a war really. The athletes in that room had a great deal of pride. We had pushed ourselves and paid the price because we abhorred losing. No one in that room wanted to be remembered as part of a team that couldn't lose to the Russians but did!

As I sat there sipping a beer, I thought about what Team Canada had accomplished. We had started out as individuals and come together as a team to win the series. We never would have won if all the players hadn't pulled together. Everyone in that room had made a contribution, and as I looked around, I reflected on how each player had helped the team to make a sensational comeback. I thought about a guy like Gary Bergman. I'd played with Gary in Detroit and knew what kind of defenceman he was. His performance in the series demonstrated that Bergie had been underrated for a long time. Not fancy maybe, but he was extremely effective at shutting down the Russian attack. Stay-at-home blue liners don't often get the credit they deserve, but now everyone would recognize Bergie's talents.

I looked at Bobby Clarke and saw a young guy who was already a leader. His work ethic was infectious, and it was easy to see that one day soon he would be the NHL's most valuable player. As I recalled how much Ronnie Ellis and I didn't want him on our line, I had to laugh.

I glanced at Ken Dryden and saw a goalie who played some super hockey in his last two games. Kenny showed why he was a winner. Before he was through he would help the Montreal Canadiens snare six Stanley Cups. I think Dryden made the fastest length-of-ice dash for a goalie in the last minute of the series. He scooted out of the net to join the celebration when I scored and then cried, "Holy smoke! There's still 34 seconds to play!" Then he raced back to his net and held the Soviets off.

While I was sitting there mulling over the series of a lifetime, my Leaf teammate Brian Glennie came over and gave me a bear hug. He didn't play against the Russians, but he stayed with us the entire time. All of the guys who played valued the support of the people who never got to suit up. It meant a lot to us.

The players didn't say much after that last game. Sure,

we hugged one another savouring the moment, but words didn't seem necessary. The sense of satisfaction was indescribable.

While the Russians had brought out the best in us because they were such a great team, they could never match our emotional intensity, nor our desire to win. That was one of the distinct differences between the two teams. Later, a reception was given for both teams before we left Moscow, but only three or four Russians showed up. I suppose it was their way of protesting the way we played. Their players couldn't believe how vicious we were. Nor could they comprehend our win-at-any-cost attitude.

One of the Russians who did attend the reception was goalie Vladislav Tretiak. Even though we scored a few more goals against him in Moscow, I never got the impression he was weakening. He was a terrific goaltender who robbed us many times and forced us to take shots from bad angles. I told an interpreter to tell Tretiak how impressed I was with his play during the entire series. Tretiak replied that I was lucky to score the goals I did, especially the last one. My emotions were still running high, so I was in no mood to hear that. I looked him straight in the eye and told him what he could do with his comments. Tretiak understood exactly what I said; no interpreter was required.

The fact is, I was very fortunate to score those game-winning goals, particularly when you consider the highly improbable circumstances. I think if someone had written a script before the series similar to what actually happened, no one would have believed it. I know I wouldn't have.

The funny thing was, we had little or no idea how people back home were reacting to the series. We did receive thousands of telegrams, letters, and postcards in Moscow from Canada, which we taped to our dressing room walls, but we were completely unaware of the coast-to-coast fever that had gripped our countrymen during the series. The moment the final goal was scored is forever etched in the mind of every Canadian who watched that last game from Moscow.

After the eighth game, someone in the dressing room asked me, "Do you have any idea what you've done? You just wrote yourself into the history books." At the time I honestly didn't give it much thought. Athletically I knew this was the highlight of my career. I think most if not all of the players on Team Canada felt the same way. I had also proved I could play hockey with the best in the world. Now I just wanted to go home, relax, and enjoy the moment for a while. I had no idea what awaited me back home.

5

Aftermath

"Can you believe it?" Eleanor asked when I found her in the crowd at Toronto's ultramodern city hall. The rain poured down relentlessly, but 80,000 people couldn't have cared less. They had come to welcome Team Canada, and not even a hurricane would have stopped them.

I should have guessed what was in store for us when we landed in Montreal. Prime Minister Trudeau and Mayor Jean Drapeau were there to greet us, along with a massive crowd. The airport was a madhouse, which went even crazier when we circled the tarmac in fire engines.

All the way back from Europe I'd felt a certain melancholy over the realization that it was all over and my teammates and I would soon be going our separate ways. Our wives had returned to Canada earlier because we had stopped over in Prague to play an exhibition game with the Czechs, which ended up tied 4-4. I didn't play in that game due to a groin injury I suffered in the final Soviet confrontation.

Eleanor was right, though. As I surveyed the thousands jammed into Nathan Phillips Square, I couldn't really believe what was happening. We had been booed and written off. The past month had been alternately frustrating and exhilarating. As I looked out into the crowd, I knew the perseverance and hard work had been worth it. Until that moment I'd had no real idea how significant our win had been for Canadians. But you could see it in their eyes. There was such happiness and excitement. People just wanted to touch you. I could feel the waves of emotion pouring over me. Then Tony Esposito and Alan Eagleson lifted me onto their shoulders as I was introduced to the crowd. I waved and thought to myself, Don't these people realize it's pouring out there? Then we sang "O Canada" together, a special moment that I'll never forget.

Once the reception was over I thought everything would soon return to normal. Was I ever wrong. As Eleanor and I drove home to Mississauga, I began to realize that the celebration had just begun. Our neighbours had rented a neon sign and placed it on our front lawn. In bright lights it read Home of Paul Henderson. People were waiting for us as we came down the road. Some had made up their own signs, which were all over our house and lawn.

In the days that followed it seemed as if every television and radio station wanted to do an interview. The Liberal Party, which was in the middle of a federal election campaign, wanted me to join them as a platform guest, a request I declined. I had expected the attention from the media and other public figures, but it seemed now as if everyone had something to say.

Once, when I halted my car at a stoplight close to home, a man jumped out of his vehicle and demanded an autograph on the spot. Then the light turned green and the other drivers started honking. But the autograph hound shook his fist at them and yelled "It's Paul Henderson." He wouldn't leave until I signed. I couldn't go to the grocery store without being approached. Everywhere I turned somebody wanted to talk to me or get an autograph. The phone never stopped ringing, even though I had an unlisted number. Cars would cruise up and down our street, hoping for a glimpse of Paul Henderson or to get a picture and autograph.

Those people who couldn't see me in person wrote letters and sent telegrams. Although I read as many of the letters as I could, I had to hire a secretary to help out. I averaged about 40 letters a day, most of which were thank-you notes. Many of them commented on what the goal had meant to them. Most wanted an autographed photo. I wish I could have sent a personal reply to each, but there just wasn't enough time. Later we developed a standard reply and included a personally signed photograph.

As a Maple Leaf, I was used to getting a fair amount of mail, but never anything like the torrent I got in the months after the series. Many people took the time to send me gifts. One I remember in particular was a beautiful handwoven rug with the Team Canada logo on it. Sent by a young woman, the rug was about three feet wide and six feet long. I liked it so much that I still use it for the front door of our new home.

Since I was one of the more marketable players, many business opportunities arose as a result of the 1972 series. Sports Management, Inc., run by former Maple Leaf trainer Bob Haggert, looked after all my promotion deals. I had considerable respect for Haggert's judgement. He knew what I was comfortable with and what would make me uneasy. I certainly wouldn't do anything controversial or something that might hurt the family unit. I filtered all requests through Haggert, and he came back and told me which ones we should seriously consider. Haggert probably presented me with one in ten proposals. He knew enough not to bring me any of the crazier ideas.

Many entrepreneurs came after me, hoping I'd lend my name and money to their product or service. Many of the ideas were harebrained and ridiculous. Today I can't even recall the specifics, but I can still see the faces of those who hoped I'd go along with their schemes. People popped out of the woodwork. I'm sure they could have put their ingenuity and energy to better use.

Many corporations gave me gifts such as a new car, a stereo, golf clubs, and a beautiful 18-carat gold watch. I signed a good promotional deal with a hockey equipment company, a men's slacks company, and a TV rental outfit. I was also able to command a good fee for speaking engagements and personal appearances. We were doing so well that we were able to set up a holding company to handle my endorsements.

I made sure we were selective. We chose the deals that required the least amount of time. For example, taking one day to shoot a commercial was fine. On the other hand, if someone wanted six or eight appearances we likely told them we weren't interested. My family time was too important to lose any of it. I played hockey in the winter and wanted to keep my summers free. However, I knew I had to take advantage of these opportunities now so that I would be able to enjoy my retirement from hockey a whole lot more. Having financial security was something I took seriously. I could probably handle any amount of money, but I'm smart enough not to tempt myself. I don't want to be too wealthy. I've seen the pitfalls.

When I think of all those money-making schemers who approached me back then, I also stop to remember people like the young lady who made me the handwoven rug. A gift like that doesn't have high monetary value, yet it was special to her. People like that would just send me items because they got caught up in the excitement of the whole thing. Along with those who wanted to take advantage of my newfound status were some very nice people who just wanted to say thanks without any benefit to themselves. These people are the people I'll remember most.

With so much going on around me I came to appreciate my family more than ever. Eleanor was happy and excited for me. She knew what happened in Moscow was going to be the highlight of my career. With the Maple Leafs there was little chance of winning the Stanley Cup, so, like me, she enjoyed the flow of those wonderful days after I scored the winning goal. Whatever happened to one of us also affected the other, and Eleanor and I went through this period of great attention together, just as we had everything else since our teens.

One of the reasons our marriage had stood the test of time is that we have 100 percent commitment to each other. Thoughts of divorce have never been part of the deal. To be sure, I've had a much easier ride than Eleanor. When I started to receive such an inordinate amount of attention after the 1972 series, she was the one who kept me on an even keel. If I got too irritated, she helped put everything back into perspective.

In terms of what we need as a family I've relied heavily on Eleanor. Whenever she says something regarding the family, I'm quick to listen. If I hear what our children say, she hears what they mean. After the 1972 series, my family helped me preserve my sanity. Whenever I thought the Cinderella story would never end, my family reminded me about the realities of life. We were always close, but the aftermath of the Canada-Soviet shoot-out probably drew us together even more.

Our daughters reacted very differently to the situation.

The eldest girl, Heather, who was nine at the time, revelled in the attention. "You want to meet my dad?" she'd ask her friends. "Line up here for interviews please." She'd hand out pictures and say, "Paul Henderson is my daddy."

Jennifer, the second oldest, who was seven at the time, had quite a different reaction. She was more on the quiet side and enjoyed the peace of home. She didn't want any of the extra attention. One time Jennifer told a reporter, "I wish my dad was a garbage collector." Jill, my youngest, was two at the time and naturally didn't have much to say at that age.

Being called a national hero had a nice ring to it. Like any other kid, I had dreamed of scoring the big goal, but I never imagined what actually transpired. Winning a Stanley Cup is without a doubt a tremendous feeling, but being remembered for a moment in time is something truly incredible. Many people recall the goal the way they remember John Kennedy's assassination or Neil Armstrong's first step on the moon. They know exactly what they were doing when I lifted the puck past Tretiak. Today I probably enjoy the adulation more than ever. I downplay the so-called "hero label," but I still find the attention very satisfying.

There was a time, though, when I wondered if I'd ever be able to sit back and enjoy the moment in peace. As a hockey player, I was used to being a celebrity of sorts, but not to the extent I was during the year that followed the 1972 series. I couldn't go anywhere without being recognized. If I was out at a restaurant, I'd hear people whisper, "There's Paul Henderson." I didn't want to stand out in a crowd. Most people would be nice and apologize about interrupting my meal for an autograph, but in their enthusiasm they'd often forget that maybe I was trying to have a nice quiet evening with my family just as they were. After three months of such attention, I was sick to death of it all.

As an NHL player, I had always enjoyed the prestige that went with being a professional athlete. Any pro has to have a bit of ego. Prior to the series, being Paul Henderson of the Maple Leafs had been enough for me. As I started to get bored with all the new fanfare, I became crusty and arrogant with people. If I was in a good mood and people treated me with respect, then there was no problem. If someone irritated me, then I might snap back at them.

I wasn't averse to trading insults with people, especially those who shoved something in my face and demanded I sign it. I could be confrontational quite easily. Some mornings I'd wake up and feel good about being the man who had scored the goal. Other days the whole business could be a real pain. People would approach me on these bad days with the best of intentions, but I just wanted to tell them to get lost. I wasn't brought up to offend people, and after a particularly nasty confrontation, I'd think to myself, Why did I act like that? Sometimes I couldn't even remember the reason why I was ticked off at someone. As I think about it now, I can see I was getting too big for my shoes.

At the time I didn't stop to think about how an athlete is seen as a role model. Athletes are rarely able to live up to the expectations of society, but they should think about what message they're sending out to young people. I had always been pretty good about signing autographs for kids. However, at this point I was getting surly and was quick to anger. Later I'd feel badly, sensing that I'd acted improperly, and soon I started asking myself why I had become so short-tempered.

I had always believed that happiness would come from success. However, after I achieved all the fame I wanted, I was probably less satisfied than I had ever been. Those days after the Canada-Russia series were a rough time for me. I seemed to have everything except peace of mind. Then something strange happened. I began a period of soul-searching, asking myself things like, What really gives purpose to life? Is that all there is? Needless to say, I couldn't come up with any answers, so I'd lie awake at night and stare up at the ceiling, trying to figure out the whole deal. A great sense of discontentment threatened to overwhelm me.

When you don't get the answers you're looking for, you start to search for other ways to release the tension. I found myself drinking more than I ever had before. True, I was never an angel, but now I found myself drowning my confusion in alcohol. You can find plenty of solace in bars filled with people in a bad mood like you. Luckily I realized I was going down the wrong road, so I stepped back before any real problems developed. I didn't like where I was going, which meant I had to take a good, hard look at myself.

I wish my father had been around then. Maybe he could have helped me deal with my emotions or given me some answers to my questions. Dad was the one who had influenced me most as a hockey player. He had believed in my potential to play professionally and had urged me to give it my best shot. He was the one who had stopped me from quitting in junior hockey. I was glad I'd followed his advice, but now he wasn't around when I needed him most. I was forced to find the answers on my own, and some days I felt terribly alone and isolated.

I started talking to people who I thought were happy. I

tried to find out if they were indeed content. Few of them would talk about what I perceived to be the important things in life. Instead, people told me what they'd like to fix. If they did this or that, then they thought they'd be truly happy. But at this point they weren't. Nobody could tell me what life was all about. Maybe when you're pursuing goals and enjoying yourself, you don't stop to think about the direction your life is actually going. I did consider myself a good father and husband. I know I wasn't perfect, but these roles were important to me and I took them seriously. I now began to think about other people beyond my family.

For perhaps the first time in my life I began to consider what people really thought of me. What about my character? What was my reputation? What about my value system? What about the ethics? What was my attitude towards people? What kind of heritage would I leave for my kids? I came to the conclusion that my value system was rather shallow. I was too worried about money and material success. I always thought about getting ahead. Most of the time the end justified the mean. I entered a whole new realm of self-examination and, quite frankly, I didn't like what I saw. It seemed as if I only had time for people who could be helpful to me somehow. What about other people? This period of reexamination changed my life forever.

While dealing with all these questions I had to go back to playing hockey for the Leafs. I worried about what people might expect from me now. What would they want from the hero of the 1972 Canada-Russia series? Could I ever live up to these expectations? I knew I had gotten a little lucky, scoring a couple of goals by being at the right place at the right time. I also knew I couldn't play hockey like Phil Esposito. I was only as good as the players I played with on the ice. You could never build a team around a player like me. I needed two good linemates to make things happen. My on-ice abilities didn't make me a leader like Darryl Sittler, Bobby Clarke, or Phil Esposito, although I knew I could be a positive influence in the dressing room and in the rink. My assets as a hockey player were clear in my mind, and I needed good players around me to bring out my attributes, since I didn't score too many goals with end-to-end rushes. I tried to keep all of this in mind, but I have to admit I got carried away at times and more than once would get in over my head.

Coming off a 38-goal season on the previous year, I had high expectations, anyway. After the Canada-Russia series, the expectations rose a little higher. The internal pressure mounted, and as it did, I tried to do things on the ice that were beyond my capabilities. I could sense an air of anticipation in the crowd whenever I got the puck. If the game was close, I'd feel the need to score the winning goal. My pride wanted me to succeed, to match the level of expectation. I'd try to talk to myself, saying, "Come on, let's be realistic. You can't do everything." The more pressure I put on myself, the more I overestimated what I could do. Later I got injured and my playing time was reduced to 40 games. From the great high in Moscow my hockey career plummetted to its lowest point in the 1972-73 season. It was a tough year to go through.

Playing hockey in Toronto means you're always under a microscope. I normally enjoyed that kind of pressure and, besides, Leaf fans knew their hockey. They could see I was giving it my best shot and seemed to sense I was having a hard time adjusting. They knew my limitations as well as I did, and I think I maintained their respect throughout this difficult period. When you play hockey in Toronto, you can never fade into the background. The media coverage is always intense.

All in all, though, I was treated very well by the media in Toronto. I knew they had a job to do, and I had no problem giving them some time. I don't think I was ever too difficult to deal with in terms of granting interviews. I'm not saying I always agreed with what they said or wrote, but most of the time I saw their point of view. I would only get upset when someone got the facts wrong.

In those days the players and writers got to know one another a little. If someone wrote something critical of me, I'd stop to consider who the writer was and whether I respected him as a person. If it was someone I thought highly of, I might talk to him about why he wrote such a story. Frank Orr, Milt Dunnell, Jim Proudfoot, and Jim Coleman were fine writers who had my respect. But there were others I tended to stay away from if at all possible. I tried to do this as subtly as I could, since I didn't want to get into a fight with the press, a battle no pro athlete ever wins. Overall, I have no complaints about how the media treated me. Even as I struggled after the 1972 series, they were pretty understanding and restricted their criticisms to hockey.

Naturally my newfound notoriety had the potential to cause problems between me and the Maple Leaf organization, both players and management. Most of my teammates had no trouble dealing with the hype surrounding me, although a few did seem to resent the attention I was getting. I don't think I handled the situation as well as I should have, which no doubt incensed them even more. I imagine, given my lacklustre performance that season, these jealous players were muttering things like, "Here's the Canadian hero. What's he done for us lately?" Today I think I have the sensitivity and maturity to deal with this type of mentality, but back then I'm sure I only fanned the flames.

All things considered, though, my role in the dressing room didn't change. Normally, I was a vocal guy who tried to pump up and motivate the other players. As I struggled, however, I noticed I wasn't doing this as much. In fact, I became a little withdrawn and started to internalize my growing negative feelings.

And there was a lot to be negative about with the World Hockey Association starting up. The Maple Leafs had enough problems without having a new league poach its players. Mind you, Toronto and the rest of the NHL clubs didn't take the WHA very seriously. Harold Ballard, who had taken over as majority owner of the Leafs in 1971, refused to believe the new league would last. However, before long we lost Rick Ley, Brad Selwood, Jim Dorey (traded to the Rangers because he signed with the WHA), Guy Trottier, Jim Harrison, and Bernie Parent. In one fell swoop the WHA decimated our entire team!

I could see that this was going to happen. I was so concerned about the situation that I approached management and begged them to sign these players. For about $10,000 to $15,000 each the Leafs could have signed all of the guys they lost. Bernie Parent was worth everything he was asking for. Any team that wants to win a Stanley Cup needs a great goalie. But the Leaf management was too arrogant to listen to me or anyone else, and it was impossible to get NHL-calibre players developed overnight to make up for such a loss. So, because of Ballard's indifference, the Leafs found themselves in deep trouble. Of course, that was only the beginning of a long night of frustration and folly for the once-great franchise, one it still hasn't fully emerged from.

When I first came to Toronto, Harold Ballard had a rather low profile. He didn't have a say in day-to-day hockey decisions and generally stayed in the background, acting more like a paid fan of the team. He had no notoriety at that point, but there were still plenty of stories circulating about him. I was very impressed by his wife, Dorothy, a really fine lady. Sadly she died of cancer in 1969, and Ballard was never the same. Had she lived she would have kept him in line. In some ways her death was the demise of Harold Ballard.

Ballard's ego grew as he took over the Leafs, following the death of his partner Stafford Smythe. He quickly became loud and obnoxious. Accountable to no one, he acted as if he were a god. The more power he got, the more money he made, the less he respected the people who worked for him. He believed a man should be judged by how much money he could make or how much publicity he could generate. To me these weren't criteria to earn respect, something that can't be bought no matter how much money you have or how famous you are.

I don't think the people who worked for Ballard can be blamed for the sorry state of the Leafs. People such as Jim Gregory, Johnny McLellan, and later Roger Neilson tried to do their jobs, but everything hinged on Ballard's moods. One day he would agree to something and the next he'd change his mind completely. If you look at Ballard's behaviour over the years, you see a man constantly shifting positions. He was consistent about one thing, though: he always got his way.

Ballard did some very good things for the community, but on the whole he treated people like garbage. Players, coaches, managers, and fans all suffered because of him. On occasion he'd lead you to believe he wanted the Leafs to win, and down deep he probably did, but he was just as interested in seeing his name in the newspaper, which was no way to run a hockey team.

Over the years Ballard had his share of confrontations with many players. I was no different. After the 1972 Canada-Russia series, both my agent Alan Eagleson and I thought this would be a good time to negotiate with Ballard for a future contract. We had to strike the iron while it was hot. Ballard seemed proud about the Leaf players doing so well in the series, so I didn't anticipate any problems in getting a new deal.

However, as we tried to negotiate, Ballard fell into one of his cantankerous moods and became impossible to deal with. Then we had to wait a year while he served a one-year prison term for his financial dealings. Meanwhile the Leafs sagged badly in 1972-73, finishing fifth in the East Division. Our 64 points put us ahead of only the Vancouver Canucks and the New York Islanders. After the great high of Moscow, I had the worst year of my NHL career. I hurt my groin again and played in just 40 games, scoring 18 goals. At this point I was in the mood for a change, and the WHA presented a tantalizing chance to escape the Gardens' zoo.

When I first heard about the new league, it didn't interest me at all. But as I got more frustrated with the Leafs, the WHA started to look better, especially the kind of money they were throwing around. I was making $75,000 at the time, and the WHA was paying out more money to players who couldn't even make it in the NHL! I saw the way Ballard treated Dave Keon, a player who gave his heart and soul to the Leafs. Yet Ballard had a hard time finding $100,000 for one of his best players. Obviously things didn't look good for me.

6

Breakaway to the WHA

"Whatever you're making," John F. Bassett told me over the telephone one day, "I'll double it and give you a five-year, no-trade contract.

"Are you serious?" I blurted, slightly stunned.

"My word is good," he replied. "I'm *very* serious."

Johnny Bassett was the owner of the Toronto Toros, one of the teams in the upstart World Hockey Association. I put him in touch with Alan Eagleson, my agent, who negotiated a $50,000 signing bonus and a personal guarantee that the contract would be paid in full by Bassett and his partner John Craig Eaton should anything happen to the team or league. Johnny F. was a wonderful man. His word was his bond and every contract he signed was honoured no matter who the player was or how he played. Players on other teams weren't so fortunate, particularly when franchises were transferred or folded.

Besides the great salary, contract guarantee, and signing bonus, Bassett threw in performance clauses keyed to my final year with the Maple Leafs. With a deal like that, who could pass it up? So I signed on the dotted line, with the intention of starting with the Toros in the 1974-75 season. In retrospect, though, I shouldn't have made the deal with Bassett until my Leaf contract expired. There was a lack of integrity on my part when I agreed to bonus money from Johnny F. based on my final season with the Leafs. If I had the chance, I'd do it differently now. What made matters worse was that Bassett ran into Ballard at a cocktail party and let it slip that I would be a Toro in a year's time. Ballard didn't like that one bit, which led to one last confrontation between us.

Harold was determined not to lose any more players to the WHA, so he came to me and asked about what he had heard from Bassett. I told him all the conditions of the Toros' offer. He then asked to meet with me and Alan Eagleson. The meeting took place at the Hot Stove League in the Gardens. Arrogantly Ballard put a contract in front of me and growled, "Here's your five-year contract, same money, but no signing bonus. Sign here!" He made it sound as if he were doing me a favour.

I looked him straight in the eye and replied, "Harold, you take this contract and shove it!"

He stared at me, rage in his eyes. But I wasn't going to back down. My mind was made up. Then, suddenly, he got up, kicked his chair over, and stormed out.

I can't say I was proud of the way I acted. I was vindictive towards Ballard, bitter and insulted for the way he treated me and the team. Still, I have to admit that it felt good to tell Harold where to go, even though I wish I'd been able to rise above the situation and just walk away, which would have been the smart thing to do.

Over the years since my retirement from hockey I tried to make up with Ballard, but he never relented. In 1981 at the Canada Cup in Montreal I saw Ballard and Clancy sitting in the Forum, watching a workout. I decided to go over and talk to him. I had a nice chat with Clancy, but Ballard didn't listen to a word I said. As time passed, he grew more spiteful, even preventing me from getting a job with Telemedia to do colour on Leaf radio broadcasts for home games in 1981. I tried to see him at his office, but he refused. I wrote to him, but he never answered. A few years later I was at a Leaf morning practice when I went into the dressing room to continue a conversation with Russ Courtnall. Ballard saw me and told Bob Stellick to kick me out. I could tell Stellick was embarrassed, so I left quietly and didn't return to the building until after Ballard's death.

In 1973-74, my final season with the Leafs, I bounced back with 24 goals and 31 assists in 69 games. We finished fourth in the East Division with 86 points. Red Kelly was the new coach, and he and I didn't quite see eye to eye. Red was a fine gentleman; we just couldn't get on the same wavelength. After my blowup with Ballard, Red benched me for a few games and kept me off the power play so I wouldn't make any of the bonus money the Toros had promised. Although I'm sure this was done under instructions from Ballard, it didn't endear me to Red at the time.

One night, when the Oakland Seals were in town, Red told me I wasn't going to dress. He said he wanted me to do some wrist curls in the weight room because he thought my wrists were a little weak. I told the general manager, Jim Gregory, about this and he just shook his head. Norm Ullman looked at me as if he couldn't believe what I was saying. Imagine, after all these years I now had weak wrists! They could have come up with something better. Today Red and I get along fine and I have considerable respect for him as one of the NHL's greatest players.

Boston wiped us out in the playoffs in four games straight that season. This series emphasized one problem in my time with the Leafs. We were never physically

tough enough to take on an opponent like Boston. I remember when the Canadiens' John Ferguson went into
Boston and took on Bruin tough guy Ted Green. After
Ferguson won the battle, Montreal owned the Bruins. I
noticed in later years how much better the Leafs played
with guys like Tiger Williams and Dan Maloney, especially on the road.

A big plus for the Leafs was the addition of Borje Salming and Lanny McDonald. Salming had loads of talent
and went on to have a long career with the Leafs. He
could really handle the puck and move it up the ice
quickly. Lanny showed all kinds of potential, but he certainly took some hard checks in his rookie season. We
tried to teach him how to protect himself after he took a
shot, and because Lanny wanted to play so badly, he was
willing to learn. Of course, he ended up with 500 goals
and a Stanley Cup ring as the captain of the Calgary
Flames. That year the Leafs also added players such as
Ian Turnbull, Errol Thompson, Inge Hammarstrom, and
Rick Kehoe. All of these guys had the makings of a team
that could be built around Darryl Sittler.

Although I could see some new hope for the Leafs, I
can honestly say my departure from the team was one of
the best things I ever did. For my family and health I
needed to get a breath of fresh air. The last two years
with the Leafs were so bad that I had developed an ulcer.
It wasn't just Ballard, but a combination of factors that
made me want to pack my bags for good. After the Canada-Russia series, I received enough attention to last me a
lifetime. I didn't need the spotlight anymore.

Those two years before I joined the WHA were dark
days for me. However, when I emerged from the black
cloud that had enveloped me despite the adulation after
the 1972 hockey summit, I was a new person, one who

was much stronger, a man whose outlook on life had changed radically. During the transition period, I learned a great deal about people. They came at me from all directions, exposing every facet of human nature and providing me with the experience that would help prepare me for the work I do today.

Shortly after I joined the Toronto Toros, I had a conversation with Frank Mahovlich, one of my new teammates. Frank helped me put the Leafs into perspective. I told him that I might one day regret leaving the team and the NHL.

"Forget it," he said. "They'll never win with him [Ballard] there."

Without thinking I asked, "What if they got a top general manager and coach?"

"Even if they get the right people, he won't let them do their job."

Obviously Frank was a better soothsayer than I was. When the Leafs got close under Roger Neilson, Ballard still managed to blow a great situation. Who can forget how Ballard treated Neilson, one of the premier coaches in the game?

I decided to enjoy the WHA and make the most of it, even if it wasn't the NHL and the Toros weren't the Maple Leafs. By the time I joined the new league in 1974-75, it was about to begin its third season and had garnered a lot more credibility with the Winnipeg Jets' signing of Bobby Hull to a million-dollar contract. People like J. C. Tremblay, Bernie Parent, Gerry Cheevers, and Derek Sanderson only added to the respectability of the new kid on the block. When Sanderson, who was a good hockey player but not a superstar, got a pile of cash to leave the Boston Bruins for the Philadelphia Blazers, you had to take notice.

What made my deal with Bassett really sweet was the fact that the Toros were now in Toronto, having moved from Ottawa. I wanted to stay in Toronto because we were comfortable there and enjoyed the area. To make a great situation even better, the Toros moved from Varsity Arena to the Gardens. I couldn't ask for anything more.

My first assignment for the WHA was to play the Russians in another eight-game series scheduled for September 1974. Only two years had passed since the first hockey summit, and I had no desire to play the Soviets again. However, I recognized the need for the WHA to showcase its talent. We had to demonstrate that the league was competitive and credible. Coach Billy Harris told us the new series would just be a series of games. There would be none of the win-at-any-cost mentality of 1972, and I made a vow that I'd never let myself get as uptight and intense as I had two years earlier. Billy's attitude took the pressure off and made playing the Russians much easier mentally.

We got off to a good start against the Soviets, tying the first game in Montreal 3-3 and winning the second 4-1 in Toronto. Before the third game in Winnipeg Harris made five major lineup changes and we lost 8-5, possibly because there was too much tinkering with the team for this level of competition. Mind you, I'm not blaming Billy Harris. At the outset he insisted that everybody would play. Still, we lost our intensity, blew a 5-3 lead in Vancouver late in the third period, and had to settle for a 5-5 draw. Over in Moscow we managed to get one tie (4-4 in the seventh game), while losing three.

I think I probably played as well in the 1974 series as I had in 1972, but I just couldn't get any goals. I played on a line with Bruce MacGregor and Mike Walton, which was a pretty good combination. My best game was in

Winnipeg when I scored twice and earned one assist. With all the chances I had throughout the series I should have scored more, but Tretiak had my number this time, as did the rest of the Soviet team. However, I was generally pleased with my performance and thought our guys proved they could play against the Soviets, who I'm sure found the series no cakewalk.

The 1974 Team Canada had a pretty loose approach to the series. When we got on the ice, we wanted to win, but the hunger wasn't the same as in 1972. Nor was the country behind this effort as it had been two years before. In order to play against the Russians you have to have fire in your belly. Unfortunately we didn't.

One of the highlights of that series was having Gordie Howe as a teammate again. He and his two sons Mark and Marty played for the Houston Aeros in the WHA, and all three were selected for Team Canada. The occasion gave me one more chance to see Gordie's legendary method of justice on ice.

In Moscow one of the Russian players took a run at Mark, nailing him with a pretty good shot. Gordie saw what happened and took note of Gennady Tsygankov, number seven. I knew what was coming. I watched carefully from the bench when Gordie went after the player who had hit Mark. The Russian picked up the puck on the far side of the rink against the boards, then started to go around his own net to begin a rush, with Gordie in hot pursuit. Tsygankov started to beat Howe to the outside when Gordie brought his stick down very sharply on the Soviet's forearm. Right away I knew the man's forearm was broken. The next day we saw Tsygankov with a substantial cast. There was no way Gordie was going to let anyone get away with hitting one of his boys!

The other nice aspect to the 1974 series was the time I

was able to spend exploring the Soviet Union. Being a history buff, I was interested in visiting their museums and libraries and looked forward to sight-seeing and taking in the ballet. I was so much more relaxed than in 1972 that when Billy Harris told me I wasn't going to play in the last game, I had no objection, since it gave me more time to tour the country.

My first year in the WHA saw the Toronto Toros finish second in the Canadian Division with 88 points, a little behind the Quebec Nordiques. I played most of the year on a line with Wayne Dillon and Tom Simpson. The latter had the hardest shot in hockey. In fact, he became the first pro hockey player in Toronto to score over 50 goals in one season. We nicknamed him "Shotgun Tom" because of his heavy shot. More than once I saw him score goals from outside the blue line, something even Bobby Hull with his powerful drives couldn't do. Simpson was a good example of a player who could have made it in the NHL if he'd had more discipline off the ice. Away from the game he was known as "Shot Glass."

I racked up 30 goals and 33 assists in 58 games that season and had a great time. We played many of our home games on Friday and Sunday nights, and coach Billy Harris would usually give us Saturday off if we won Friday night. One of the country's major breweries gave out silver tankards to the star of the game, and I won the award about eight times. So, after the game on Friday, Eleanor and I would pile the kids into the car and head to our family home near Goderich, Ontario. There we'd do some horseback riding and, in the winter, a little skidooing. Then we'd head back to Toronto on Sunday morning. It was incredible to have a few Saturdays off during the hockey season so I could enjoy activities with my family!

The Toros had some pretty good hockey players. Frank Mahovlich had signed on after ending his NHL days with Montreal. Frank was in the twilight of his career, but he was still great to watch. When Frank was flying, he was poetry in motion. He was so talented that he could score whenever he wanted. Vaclav Nedomansky, a big Czechoslovakian, was a very talented centre. He scored 40 goals for us and could do just about anything on ice. In goal we had Gilles Gratton, one of the great all-time characters in hockey. He believed he was reincarnated and acted like it. Gratton didn't have a long career because no team would put up with his antics. One of the more printable Gratton stories was the time he showed up on the ice for practice wearing only a pair of skates and gloves. And he was the goalie! Despite his totally different personality, he was very talented musically. When we were in the Soviet Union, he listened to the Russian national anthem just once and then sat down and played it perfectly on the piano!

Under Billy Harris we had a record of 22-17-1 when he was fired by the Toros. The year before Harris had won 43 games and the team had gone on to the semifinals. Billy was a very knowledgeable hockey man. I had great respect for him as a coach, but some people thought we should have won more. Eventually this feeling cost Billy his job, but in my opinion it wasn't his fault that we didn't have a tough enough team or that our defence struggled most nights. The San Diego Mariners, a team that played like the Philadelphia Flyers in their Broad Street Bully days, beat us in the first round of the playoffs in six games.

A freak accident knocked me out of the last part of the season and the playoffs. We were playing Phoenix at the Gardens and I was headed to the bench for a line change.

One of their players, who was also heading to his bench, banged his knee against mine. I didn't think there was anything wrong, but when I jumped over the boards for my next shift, my knee gave out. I couldn't put any weight on it. As soon as the team doctor looked at it, he told me I had torn my knee ligaments. After surgery I had to wear a cast from hip to toe. When you're in a full-length cast, you start having doubts about your career. Without good knees it's difficult to do all the things you normally do on the ice. Just think what Bobby Orr might have been able to achieve if he could have played his entire career with good knees. Luckily, though, my injury wasn't as bad as Bobby's.

We started the next season, 1975-76, with a new coach, Bobby Baun. Bobby was an honest, straightforward man, but we really didn't have a competitive team and as a result finished last in the Canadian Division. Baun was replaced by Gilles Leger before the year was out. Mark Napier was a great addition to the Toros. Fresh from the junior Toronto Marlies, he started slowly but came on to score 43 goals and 93 points, definite signs of a star hockey player.

Our poor season finished the Toros in Toronto. There was no way they could compete with the Maple Leaf tradition. The Leafs, no matter how they are doing, are always the talk of the town. People live on the hope that one day they'll return to form. This was a loyalty the Toros could never overcome in spite of some serious efforts. So, from the hockey hotbed of Toronto, the team decided to move to Birmingham, Alabama. Talk about a difference in atmosphere!

Even though my contract stipulated I didn't have to go if the team moved more than 50 miles from Toronto, I was happy to leave. Toronto had been great for me and my family, but by 1976 I was ready for a change of scenery.

I'll always remember my first trip to Birmingham. I went with Eleanor and Frank Mahovlich in the middle of July to check things out before the start of the season. When we walked off the plane, it must have been over 100 degrees Fahrenheit. I turned to Eleanor and said, "No man or beast can survive in this weather."

We gave Birmingham a chance, though, and fell in love with the place. The city had built a beautiful new hockey rink in spite of an economic depression in the South at the time. We changed the team nickname from Toros to Bulls and drew about 11,000 fans per game, which wasn't bad, considering Alabama wasn't exactly a hockey stronghold. What I loved most, though, were the people. My family and I got involved in the community largely through church activities, which were an important part of life in an area traditionally known as the "Bible Belt." Soon we made some really good friends and ended up building a home there, which we kept until recently.

Since nobody knew who I was down there, I could go almost anywhere and not be recognized. My wife was no longer Mrs. Paul Henderson; now she became known as Eleanor. I could play golf and tennis year-round and I even bought myself a dirt bike, which I'd take out into the country and ride forever. I must have put about 4,000 miles on that bike in two years.

By 1977-78 the WHA was down to a league of eight teams. Under new coach Glen Sonmor we improved by nine points to finish sixth and earn the final playoff spot, but Winnipeg beat us out in five games. I had my best year statistically in the WHA, with 37 goals and 66 points. Suddenly I found myself on a team filled with tough guys. Dave Hanson, Steve Durbano, Frank Beaton,

Gilles Bilodeau, Pat Westrum, and Serge Beaudoin were all willing fighters. Four of them ended the season with over 200 minutes in penalties each and none of them played more than half a season! Sonmor was a real players' coach, so these guys would do whatever he asked, and Glen didn't mind watching them get into scraps.

Naturally I got plenty of room on the ice. When you have a tough team as we did, the opposition isn't too interested in starting trouble. If anyone took a run at any of our players, the guy was soon surrounded by five of our players. It got so bad that I heard some of our opponents couldn't eat their pregame meal when they played us. In fact, if somebody ran into me, they'd apologize! Sonmor never had to say a word when trouble erupted on the ice. Instantly he'd have at least seven guys look back at him, waiting for his approval to go after somebody. On other teams I played with the coach would glance down his bench when trouble brewed and nobody would look him in the eye. What bothered me were the guys on our team who all of a sudden got brave because they had tough players to back them up. I had never played the game that way in the NHL, and I wasn't going to give out any cheap shots now. Since I was one of the oldest players, the guys were quick to watch out for me. I certainly enjoyed the extra space I got on the ice to play my game and finally realized how Gordie Howe must have felt all those years when nobody dared to check him.

One Thanksgiving night we were at home to Cincinnati. At about the 12-second mark a full-scale brawl broke out. The newspapers called it the Thanksgiving Day Massacre, and that pretty well described it. The whole affair took at least an hour to clear up, during which time I stopped about five or six fights. Often that season I acted as a peacemaker, hoping to prevent someone from getting killed. Since I didn't have to fight, I could stand back and watch these boys go at it. Pound for pound, we had some of the toughest players in hockey. They were great with their dukes, and I was happy they were on my side.

Steve Durbano was one of the wilder and crazier guys. He came to us after five seasons in the NHL with four different teams and over 1,000 penalty minutes. In one year with the Bulls Steve played in a mere 45 games and racked up 284 penalty minutes. Steve and his wife at the time, Lisa, were totally unlike Eleanor and me, yet somehow we got along. We were a quiet, reserved couple who lived a Christian lifestyle; they were totally unpredictable and at the other end of the spectrum.

Steve and Lisa fought constantly and would scream at each other all the time. Still, they were often a funny couple to watch. The first time I met this fractious pair was at a team Thanksgiving dinner. Steve was telling us about how he had "invested a few thousand dollars in this marriage." We weren't quite sure what to make of this, so Steve said, "Honey, show them." Lisa pulled up her sweater, and, without a bra on, the "investment" was clear. There are certainly some talented surgeons out there!

When the team went on a road trip, Steve would leave his car with his wife. Lisa wasn't the greatest driver in the world, and when we got back from a trip, Steve would show up at practice with a car full of fresh dents. Eventually we dubbed the car "the Dentmobile."

The next season, 1978-79, John Brophy was named coach. Considering his reputation, I thought things would get even wilder than they were. To my surprise, everyone seemed to settle down a little. Brophy and I hit it off right away. He gave me all the ice time I wanted. I was on the power play, killed penalties, and took regular shifts. Brophy was the type of coach who would put up with anything if he felt you were trying your best. He knew I came to play and always gave him 100 percent. Since I didn't have any performance clauses in my contract, he also knew all my efforts were for the good of the team.

When Brophy came across a player who had the talent but wasn't putting in the effort, he couldn't handle the situation. Hockey was his whole life. John was totally immersed in the game. He was 45 years old in 1978, and I still would have put him out against anybody in the league. His level of physical fitness was incredible. They didn't come any tougher than John Brophy. He had played his entire career in the minors, and to many of the players who never made it to the big leagues, he was a legend. They loved him, and I suppose those he played against hated to meet Brophy when he was in a bad mood. I know I wouldn't have wanted to skate against the man.

Maybe many people don't know this, but Brophy had a great side to him. He'd stand up and die for one of his players, especially someone who worked hard for him. Once, in an interview, he said he respected me as a person because I came to play every night. When I was thrown out of the Gardens by Ballard, Brophy, who was coaching the Leafs at the time, took me aside and said, "Paul, my door is always open for you anytime." I'll never forget that.

I was glad Brophy got a chance to coach in the NHL. Unfortunately Toronto was the worst place for him. I knew he'd be in a terrible spot if the team started losing which, of course, it did. He might have had more success in another city where the spotlight wasn't quite so glaring.

Our team in Birmingham became known as the "Baby Bulls" because we had so many young players. Bassett raided the junior ranks and signed many 18-year-olds, including Rick Vaive, Rob Ramage, Craig Hartsburgh, Michel Goulet, Gaston Gingras, and Pat Riggin. Brophy and I would sit on the team bus sometimes and talk about these young kids. "Imagine what they'll be like in three or four years," we'd say. They were a little wild and just learning to play the game, but the potential was amazing. Most of these players went on to have great NHL careers. Our future as a team, though, was pretty clear. We won 32 games and finished in last place in what turned out to be the WHA's final season.

The six teams left at the end could have survived since they had solid financing behind them. However, the reason many of the owners were in the WHA was because they hoped to get into the NHL one day, which was exactly what happened to Edmonton, Winnipeg, Quebec, and Hartford in 1979-80.

Since my contract was guaranteed, I never worried about the constant turmoil suffered by the WHA teams. At times, though, it wasn't easy to concentrate on hockey. The Birmingham Bulls weren't a great draw on the road. We'd go into places like Houston, Phoenix, and San Diego and find hardly any fans there. I could easily have a conversation with an opponent on the ice and not think twice about it. There was no pressure and practically no media attention. One time when we were in Phoenix to play the Roadrunners a bunch of us rented dune buggies and went out for a ride in the desert on a game day! We had a crazy time rolling those vehicles through the sand. Activities like that made visiting these cities one of the pleasures of playing in the WHA.

If I had been a tough guy or fighter, the WHA might

not have been so much fun. Often the league seemed more like Roller Derby on skates. We had a lot of tough guys who would fight at the drop of a hat. The fans, especially those in the South, loved those wild nights where the fighting was more important than the game. I was just thankful I didn't have to fight. I wouldn't have lasted long.

Being a fighter isn't an easy way to earn a living in hockey. Once a tough guy can't or won't fight anymore he has no choice but to retire. Fighters usually know when they've come to the end of the line, and so does the opposition. Like sharks, they can smell the blood. Everyone you've ever beaten up comes after you, and there's no escape. Some fighters refuse to acknowledge their fighting days are over and hang around too long, something that happened to Dave Schultz and Dave Semenko. They didn't win too many fights when their careers were drawing to a close. One night I remember Eddie Shack being chased all over the ice. Eddie was a good hockey player, but he made many enemies on the way up, and they turned on him when they got the chance. There's always a new young gun who wants to make a name for himself, and what better way than to beat up a former tough guy?

Most players don't really like to fight. In my last year with the Leafs a kid named Bob Neely joined the team. He came with a fighter's reputation from the Peterborough Petes. The Leafs thought they'd solved their toughness problem for a long time, but Neely didn't want to fight. He was expected to be a physical presence on the ice, but that wasn't in his nature. Eventually the Leafs traded him to Colorado.

There are some players who enjoy fighting. I once had a conversation with current Maple Leaf captain Wendel

Clark. I had just seen a game where he'd gotten into a scrap. "Wendel, you know you're a good enough hockey player that you really don't need to fight to be effective. Why do you do it?" I asked.

"I like to fight," he told me.

I know Wendel has plenty of talent to play hockey without fighting. Most tough guys, though, aren't in such a good position. Sooner or later they won't be able to answer the bell.

If there was one man who played tough but survived for years, it was Gordie Howe. Still, when I think about it, I never saw Gordie actually get into a fight. His reputation was such that nobody challenged him, and when he destroyed the New York Rangers' Lou Fontinato with one punch in 1959, opposing players became even more wary of him. Who would want to take on a legend? Gordie probably knocked out more guys with his elbows than anybody else in the history of hockey.

I have to admit there were times when I'd see an NHL game on television and wish I was playing there. It was hard to get excited about winning the WHA's Avco Cup. Every kid grows up thinking about having his name on the Stanley Cup, not on a trophy named after a financial company! Whenever I thought about it, I found myself wishing the league would fold, since I figured I could easily get a job in the NHL.

The adrenaline would flow a little more against teams like the Quebec Nordiques and the Winnipeg Jets. Those cities took hockey seriously and put some great teams together. Quebec featured many quality French-Canadian players such as Marc Tardif, Rejean Houle, J. C. Tremblay, and Real Cloutier. The Jets not only had Bobby Hull, but also a terrific group of European players, guys like Anders Hedberg, Ulf Nillson, and Kent Nilsson. The WHA gave many fine Europeans a chance to play in North America. Another positive for the league was that it gave so many young players their first professional experience. In addition to those in Birmingham the WHA started the careers of players like John Tonelli, Mark Howe, Mike Liut, Mark Messier, and Wayne Gretzky.

Gretzky began his career with the Indianapolis Racers in 1978-79 and then moved to the Edmonton Oilers in a trade. He was just 17 and looked terribly fragile. He wasn't a dominating presence early in the season when we played against him a little more often. But his statistics started to rise, and by the end of the year he had a total of 46 goals and 100 points. It was too early to say if Gretzky would make it big at this point, but he certainly silenced the critics after he joined the NHL and became the premier player in the game. The same was true of Messier. He only scored one goal with Cincinnati in 1978-79 but later became a powerful force in the NHL.

The WHA had a revolutionary effect on hockey, much like Bobby Orr did. Orr changed the way the game was played on the ice. Defencemen became part of the offence. He also changed the game off the ice by signing an unheard of contract as a rookie and by using an agent to negotiate it for him. The new league changed the game by waking the players up to the fact that there was serious money to be made. When Bobby Hull got a million-dollar deal, we realized we had been underpaid for a long time. Most of us played hockey because we loved the game. We would have a "career" when we finished playing. When the big dollar started getting tossed around, hockey became a business. It wasn't just a game anymore. Some people refused to acknowledge the change, Harold Ballard for one. When I saw Davey Keon fighting tooth and nail for a paltry $100,000 contract, it really made me wonder. Players in the WHA who were given that kind of money couldn't even carry Keon's stick and skates. People told Ballard this, but he refused to listen, even though Keon did go back to the Leafs. (He later joined the WHA in 1975.) Many players tended to be loyal almost to a fault. I've heard Phil Esposito say that the craziest thing he ever did was to resign with the Boston Bruins when the WHA was offering more money. He wanted to finish his career in Boston. Naturally they traded him a couple of years later.

In the last two years of the WHA's existence we started to play some NHL teams during the preseason. The Atlanta Flames would come over to Birmingham to play some real barn burners with us. Although the WHA teams more than held their own against the NHL clubs, there was no doubt the older league was stronger. Their teams had much better defencemen, a fact that would tip games in their favour.

The Atlanta Flames wanted me to join their club for the 1979-80 season. My preference was to stay in Birmingham, where their farm team would be located. I came to an agreement with the Flames and general manager Cliff Fletcher in which I would play and work with the young kids in Birmingham and go to Atlanta if there were injuries. About halfway through the year they ran into problems and I got the call. I played in 30 games for Atlanta and scored seven goals.

Two of those goals were scored in my final game at Maple Leaf Gardens. On one goal I deked Leaf goalie Mike Palmateer and put a backhander just under the crossbar. My mom was sitting in the seats, and I caught her eye just as I was raising my arms to celebrate the goal. The Flames went on to defeat the Leafs 5-1, and when I was named the first star of the game, the crowd gave me a great round of applause. It was a thrill to end my last game at the Gardens on such a high note.

The Flames planned to leave Atlanta for Calgary to start the 1980-81 season. Cliff Fletcher offered me a two-year contract to play for him. He told me I'd be a role player and help out with the development of some of the youngsters on the team. Cliff has always understood the value of having veterans around. At 38 I felt I could still play in the NHL, and if the Flames had stayed in Atlanta, I would have signed. After talking it over with Eleanor, though, we decided we didn't want to move again. Birmingham was now our home.

The past 18 years had been a wonderful experience. Just as I'd hoped, I'd played hockey into my late thirties. But now it was time to get on with something new.

Was I really that young? Here I am as a Detroit Red Wing playing against Dean Prentice and goalie Eddie Johnston in Boston. (HAROLD BARKLEY)

Ballet on ice with some of the greats of the game: the St. Louis Blues' Doug Harvey *(left)* , Al Arbour, and Glenn Hall. I'm the Maple Leaf in the middle, the only guy with a helmet. (GRAPHIC)

An NHL chorus line? Leafs against the Vancouver Canucks. Dunc Wilson *(left)*, Dale Tallon, and my buddy Ron Ellis behind me. (York University Archives)

A classic battle—the Montreal Canadiens' Gilles Tremblay slams into the boards with me. (Graphic)

Game 2 of the 1972 Canada-Soviet series in Toronto. That's Ronnie behind the net and me falling to the ice. These guys were no pushovers: Valeri Kharlamov *(left)*, Vladislav Tretiak, and Alexander Ragulin. (CANADA-WIDE)

Darryl Sittler and me signing autographs at a Meet the Leafs luncheon. (TORONTO STAR/C. MCCONNELL)

En garde! Fencing with Soviet captain Viktor Kushkin —Game 3 in Winnipeg. (CANADA WIDE)

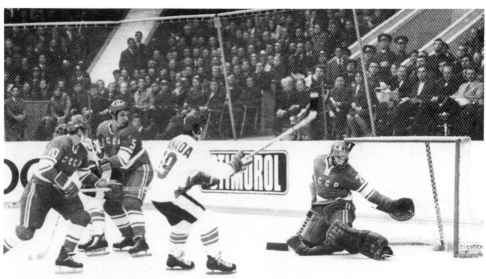

Rifling one past Tretiak was never easy. Game 5 in Moscow. Note the wire screen instead of glass, one of the many peculiarities of hockey in the USSR. (FRANK LENNON)

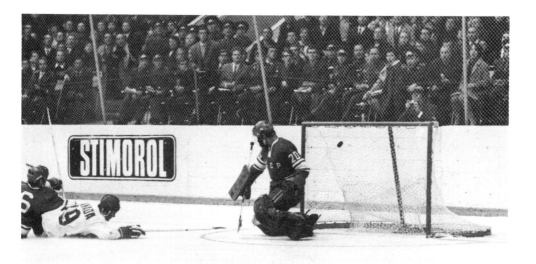

The impossible becomes real. Scoring the winning goal in Game 7. (FRANK LENNON)

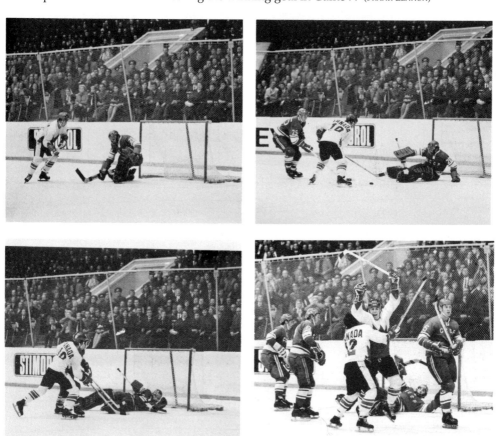

Sweet victory! The series clincher in Game 8. I know this was the most thrilling moment of my career. For one instant all Canadians were united in joy. I hope we never forget that feeling. We can sure use it today. (FRANK LENNON)

My daughters try to deal with their dad's instant celebrity after I scored the winning goal for the third straight time. Heather *(back Left)*, Jennifer *(right)*, and Jill *(foreground)*. (CANADA-WIDE)

Tony Esposito *(left)* and Alan Eagleson hoist me onto their shoulders after our return from Europe. (CANAPRESS)

Canada welcomes back its heroes in Toronto's Nathan Phillips Square. (CANADA-WIDE)

Maybe I should have been a high jumper. Screening the Phoenix Roadrunners' net as a Toronto Toro. Is that Woody the Woodpecker on the goalie's chest? (TORONTO STAR/G. BEZANT)

Another unforgettable moment for me. My final appearance at Maple Leaf Gardens in 1980, this time as an Atlanta Flame. We beat the Leafs 5-1 and I scored twice. (CANADA WIDE)

My lovely daughters today. Heather *(left)*, Jennifer, and Jill.

My grandson Joshua (Jennifer's son) having his first skate in 1988.

Grandsons Brandon *(left)* and Zachary (Heather's sons) with Eleanor and me, Christmas 1991.

Eleanor and me today.

7

Leaving the Game

"Where's all the equipment?" I asked one of the other players in the dressing room.

"Beats me," he replied.

What a way to finish my hockey career! I had stayed in Birmingham to play one more season (1980-81) for Calgary's Central League farm team. As the year wound down, it was obvious the local ownership didn't have the resources to continue. By February the decision was made to cease operations. So, one morning, we came to practice and all of our equipment was gone, a pretty good indication that the end had come.

Realistically it was going to be my last year playing hockey, anyway. I've always been able to assess myself honestly. Because I stayed in top shape physically, there was no doubt in my mind that I could still skate at the NHL level. I had even turned down the opportunity to play with the Calgary Flames. At 38 I knew I would only be a role player and likely on an occasional basis. There would be no more major parts to play. On the positive side I was leaving the game in relatively good health after a long career. I knew the time had come to walk away. This realization made the transition very easy.

That didn't mean I wouldn't miss the game I had

played for so long. Real life seldom offers what the hockey world does. For example, few things can take the place of the camaraderie you share with teammates. Half the fun of hockey is in the dressing room, kibitzing back and forth. The badgering and the great one-liners make the room a special place. I also enjoyed the physical side of the job. Working out, practising, and playing the games made hockey a great way to earn a living, not to mention the money and the lifestyle it afforded.

Early in my career the excitement was high as I tried to prove I belonged. Travelling to all the cities and meeting great players added to the air of anticipation in my first few years. In my last seasons as a professional I was much more relaxed. I spent time trying to give young players some direction without preaching to them, demonstrating a few of the tricks I'd picked up over the years. I loved the people aspect of the hockey business, and when I left the game, I knew I wanted to get a job where I could have personal contact with clients or customers. Knowing this helped make the transition to retirement a little easier because I had an area of interest.

I wasn't exactly sure where I would find my niche outside hockey, but I was certain of one thing: I would never make my living in the game once I was through playing. I had no desire to coach, scout, or manage, and thanks to Harold Ballard I didn't get the chance to try broadcasting. I wanted to do something entirely different, something challenging.

Mentally I was prepared for the changes a new career would bring into my life. Many hockey players don't find the transition so easy. When I was playing hockey, many of us didn't make very good use of our free time. For instance, we must have wasted endless hours playing cards. Amusing ourselves with card games was a very good way to stay loose and develop a good feeling among team members. Hockey players are always looking for ways to deal with the pressures of playing, but I'm sure we could have put all of those idle hours to better use developing skills that would have been helpful in the work world after retirement.

Card playing was one of the healthier pastimes. Unfortunately many players turned to drinking as a way to relieve tension. How deeply a person got involved in alcohol was his own choice, but there weren't too many players who were able to resist the temptation.

Nothing compares to the rush you feel when you're playing the game. There's no feeling like it in the world. When you're performing in front of 16,000 fans and millions more on television, it's a tremendous high. After the game, you go out and have a few beers with the guys. Soon the conquests are exaggerated and you start to think you're invincible. You'll always be young and one day the Stanley Cup will be yours.

As a player gets older, he has to learn how to deal with the notion that someday he may be rejected. I was only traded once in my career and felt a tremendous sense of rejection. Although I left the game of my own volition, I can still imagine the feeling of devastation if at 28 or 29 someone had told me, "You can't play anymore. You're not good enough." It would have been a brutal shock. After the 1991 training camp, the Leafs cut a few players around the age of 30, most if not all of whom probably felt they could still contribute. Suddenly they were gone, some to other teams, some to find a new way to make a living. It isn't surprising when players turn to alcohol as a release from dealing with these often harsh realities.

A few players get a little carried away. One of my Maple Leaf teammates, Jim McKenny, became better known for his off-ice exploits than his playing career. McKenny was a talented player, but it was his drinking adventures that made him a legend in the NHL. I would never have believed in a thousand years how life worked out for him. He has a very good job as a sportscaster at CITY-TV in Toronto and is doing quite well. Jim had the courage to go to Alcoholics Anonymous and get himself straightened out. He is also great about giving time to worthwhile causes in the community and works closely with AA, sharing his experiences with alcoholism. McKenny's story is a good one because it demonstrates that many of the wilder athletes can get their life together and make the transition to retirement when they no longer have the game to fall back on.

McKenny will also be forever known for his great one-liners. One night the Leafs were in Philadelphia to play the Flyers, who had a pretty tough team at the time. The dressing room was very quiet as we were getting ready, which prompted Guy Kinnear, one of the trainers, to say out loud, "It's as quiet as a morgue in here."

"You'd be quiet, too," McKenny shot back, "if you knew you were going to die in half an hour!"

The room broke up in laughter. The tension was gone, we'd all loosened up, and we went out and beat the Flyers. Every team needs players who have a sense of humour like McKenny's.

Unfortunately not all stories have a happy ending. Brian Spencer's life is the other side of the coin. I played with him for a couple of seasons while he was with the Leafs. Brian wasn't the most skilled player, but he had tremendous heart. A willing battler, he could spark a team with his approach to the game. He was picked up by the New York Islanders, traded to Buffalo, and then dealt to Pittsburgh. I got to know Brian when he played in Toronto. My wife and I had him and his family over for Christmas one year, and even when he went to the Islanders, he would come over to see us. Brian's father was tragically killed trying to get a local television station in British Columbia to televise a Leaf game one Saturday night. The incident affected Brian immeasurably, but his problems began when he could no longer play hockey.

With no stability in his life Brian ended up living in a trailer in a Florida swamp, associating with people he should have stayed away from. Eventually he got himself into a situation where he was charged with murder. Once he was acquitted, Brian decided to go in a new direction. He came to my office after his trial and told me he couldn't do any more physical labour. His body hurt too much. He needed a job that would give him a chance to start a new life and was even thinking of moving back to the Toronto or Buffalo area. I told him, "You have to make up your mind, Brian. Your friends, the people you hang out with, have a great influence on your life. You need to make a radical change."

Considering my associations with business people, I felt I could help him find a job. Before he left my office I told him, "If you keep your nose clean and you really want to work hard, then maybe I'll be able to help you get a job." I gave him my telephone number and told him to stay in touch. He thanked me and said he would call me later. I know Brian also asked Darryl Sittler and Rick Martin if they could help. I'm sure he was serious about making a fresh start.

Two months later Brian was murdered while back in Florida. He just couldn't stay away from certain people no matter who tried to help him. Brian's twin brother, Byron, wanted Brian to return to his native British Columbia. He warned Brian that he would end up dead if he didn't leave the wrong people behind. Brian Spencer's case may be extreme, but it is a classic example of how some players struggle when their hockey careers are over.

Many bad habits can be picked up during a player's career, and they aren't necessarily restricted to drinking. When I played in the WHA, drug use was common. One team I was on had five or six players who were regular drug users. I would worry whenever we crossed the border and went through customs. I'd make sure I was either the first to get through or the last. My impression was that drug use in the WHA was fairly widespread.

The NHL wasn't free of drug use, either. It was nothing like the WHA, but it was definitely there. In recent years some high-profile cases have become public knowledge and heavy suspensions have been handed out. When I played in the NHL, drug use was evident, but the players were more discreet and it wasn't reported in the media.

Preparing to play a game is more complex now than in my day. Players spend much more of their time at the job than ever before. When I played, we would get to the rink at 10:20 a.m. in the morning, hit the ice at 10:30, practise for about an hour, and be on a bar stool by noon. Today there is film to watch, weight room training to complete, and major rehabilitation programs to do if you're injured. Some teams also employ psychologists to help players deal with the mental side of the game. What I'd like to see, though, are formal exit programs where players are given assistance once their careers are over.

However, owners and managers today are much more aware and understanding of players' problems. I think there is a classier type of person in charge now. People like Bruce McNall and Cliff Fletcher have a genuine concern for the people who work for them, and players have more opportunities to express their opinions and give input. The situation isn't perfect, but it is far better than when I was playing in the NHL.

What irritates me most was the lack of decency on the part of many managers and owners in my day. It was their role in life to keep players down and make them feel like pieces of meat. They'd feed you a line like, "It's for the good of the team," but that never stopped them from letting you go when they thought you were used up. I remember how a former teammate, Larry Jeffrey, was treated after he was injured. He hurt his knee and the Red Wings simply discarded him. Being the consummate team player that he was, Larry often played hurt. When I saw what happened to him, it made me think about how far I would go for any team. I wanted to be around for a while, so I learned to take care of myself. I knew management wouldn't care if something happened to me.

The way Gordie Howe was treated was even more ludicrous. The Red Wings knew Gordie was the best player in the world. They also knew what the top players were earning. Did they pay him accordingly? No way. Gordie loved playing hockey so much that money was secondary. They lied and cheated the great Red Wing and fed him a line of crap. What bothers me most was that the people in management had once been Gordie's teammates! Being a little naive, Gordie once said no hockey player was worth $100,000. To a large degree superstars decide what the salaries will be. Today's players should thank Wayne Gretzky, Mario Lemieux, and Brett Hull for the salary scales now in place. You can't blame Howe, though. There was no representation in his heyday. He wanted to play hockey, pure and simple. Gordie was only 18 when he began his career in 1946 and would have given anything just to get a Red Wing jacket!

Hockey players used to be signed by the pro teams as early as 14 years of age, which was how old Bobby Orr was when he first played for the Oshawa Generals, the Bruins' junior affiliate. When you start thinking about professional hockey at such an early age, the game becomes all you really know. Back then management knew this and used it to control you. In junior a teammate of mine, Buddy Blom, a good goaltending prospect, was blackballed because he wanted to get an education. He tried to buck the system and they wouldn't let him. They wanted him to do it their way. Naturally Blom never played NHL hockey.

When I finished junior hockey, I scored 49 goals in my final season with the Hamilton Red Wings. I led the league by 13 goals and was the first all star right winger. The year before we had won the Memorial Cup. When it came time to turn pro, I got the minimum salary of $7,000 with a $1,500 signing bonus. There were no negotiations. Even though I had completed a good junior career, I had no bargaining power. They told me that was all I was getting, no questions allowed.

The pendulum has now swung the other way. Players understand hockey is a big business. They work hard to get themselves into a position where they can capitalize on contracts and endorsements. Players who have a big year in their option season can cash in on a great contract. Million-dollar-a-year deals are becoming more common in the NHL today, and players are now walking away from their teams and demanding a trade or a better pact. Who can blame them for looking after their best interests?

One way to protect yourself is to hire an agent, someone who can blow your horn a lot better than you can. Agents have the time, resources, and knowledge to deal with management on tough issues. They can play hardball for you. Of course, as in any industry, there are both good and bad agents out there. When I decided to go this route in 1970, I went for the best in the business, and at the time that meant Alan Eagleson.

I first met Eagleson when I was with Detroit. He came down to talk to us at the Royal York Hotel when we were in town to play the Leafs. Eventually we became friends. After I saw what he did for Bobby Orr, I figured there was no sense getting second best. I have no regrets about signing with Al. I did very well with him. Some players are now coming out and complaining about how Eagleson treated them and how he took their money, but I was his client for five years before he ever sent me a bill for his services. When I finally asked him to send me an invoice, he billed me for $5,000, or $1,000 a year, which was pretty good service for a small charge. My accountant today, Marvin Goldblatt, is the same accountant Eagleson had handling my financial affairs in 1970. We've had a long and agreeable relationship.

Eagleson has always been a controversial figure and the spotlight has intensified since a movement began to remove him as head of the National Hockey League Players Association. Although Al ultimately resigned as executive director of the NHLPA, he has rarely taken a step backwards. Al is very talented and incredibly adept at reading any given situation. Cocky by nature, he truly believes no one can do a job better than he can. He was a master in wielding his power and authority over the NHLPA and was able to do more for hockey than anybody else I could mention. He advanced the rights of players by organizing the union in 1967, and he put international hockey back on the map in 1972 when it was dying due to lack of interest.

I haven't always enjoyed Eagleson's methods. The way

he got things done wasn't my style. Certainly he accomplished a great deal through intimidation. Al was more than willing to steamroll over anybody or anything in his way. As a player representative, I saw Al up close in action during meetings. He would ask for our input and, after some discussion, he'd tell us to go in his direction. Usually there was no resistance because we trusted him. We leaned on him so heavily and were so intimidated that we willingly followed his advice in most cases. I have no doubt Al was trying to help us, and he did. I also know Eagleson helped himself, as well. No one has benefitted from hockey more than Alan Eagleson. To his credit, Al has never pretended that he was lily-white or lacked self-interest.

As I look back on things now, the players were wrong to let certain issues slide. We shouldn't have had the director of the NHLPA also act as an agent for players. Obviously this wasn't a smart arrangement, since it is impossible to do both jobs effectively. There are too many conflicting interests to deal with and, in effect, the players didn't control the union. We should have asked for more advice and sought outside opinions on key issues. When I would call a meeting as a player rep, not many of the players wanted to listen. They would only stay when it was absolutely mandatory. Most of them felt whatever was proposed was going to happen, anyway. They would rather go out for a beer and have a good time.

I became a player representative with the Leafs mostly at the urging of Alan Eagleson. He encouraged us to get involved. There were no particular issues I was interested in pursuing, but I did want to see what it was like to be a player rep. I attended all the meetings and contributed whenever possible, knowing full well that we needed a union to control the owners, who had far too much control over a player's life. You were always subject to the whims of management. Players would get sent down to the minors for no reason. One manager even moved players around based on his superstitions! Without some intervention by the union the players had virtually no protection.

We were hardly radical people. Most of us were born in the forties and fifties in rural Canada. We respected authority. I don't think we tried to take advantage of anyone. When we negotiated, we tried to be fair and reasonable. Our goal was to try to come up with proposals that were acceptable to both sides. Obviously we were successful at this because we never had a strike. The owners played hardball with us, and we should have been more vocal about some issues. They took advantage of us in some areas, but under the circumstances I think we did the best we could. Hindsight is always perfect.

Today many of the players of that era are bitter and upset that they didn't get a better deal, certainly with regard to their pensions. Some now voice an opinion that they should have looked at everything more critically, which is something anyone can say when things don't turn out quite as expected. The fact remains that these players had their chances but didn't do anything. And I, too, certainly wish I'd taken a much stronger stance when I had the opportunity. Eagleson put together many deals where he thought everyone was satisfied only to be made a villain when somebody came across new information. This sort of thing happened to Al many times.

The NHLPA today is in a state of transition. Bob Goodenow, the new director, has gone the extra mile to inform the players. He isn't afraid to spend the money necessary to get the proper information, and the players now get all the facts and figures they need to make a well-informed decision. I think the strike that was undertaken recently was done for philosophical reasons as much as anything. The players had to show they were serious and willing to take a stand. The owners weren't going to get away with any lies. Still, it was good to see the issue resolved before the 1992 playoffs were lost, which would have been disastrous for the game. A middle ground always has to be found for the good of hockey. Nobody wants to see teams fold and jobs lost.

Having no substantial financial worries made my retirement from hockey much easier. There was no immediate pressure to succeed, so I could take my time and see what I liked best. The first thing I tried was the brokerage business. The week the farm team folded in Birmingham I started to look into opportunities outside hockey. A friend of mine was putting an office together for E. F. Hutton, the brokerage firm, and asked if I was interested in joining the business once hockey was over. When the season came to a sudden halt in February, I went to New York to take the necessary training, and by springtime I was ready to be a full-time broker.

I looked forward to this line of work because the sales aspect had great appeal for me, not to mention the stock market itself. Since I'm a morning person, I found the hours to be ideal and the job a perfect setup. I would be in the office by 7:00 a.m. and could hit the tennis court by 4:00 p.m. In the first three months I opened up 87 accounts and was doing very well. I was as competitive and aggressive a broker as I ever was as a hockey player. As it turned out, though, I wasn't in the brokerage business for long, but I enjoyed myself while I was.

What ultimately ended my new career was the difficulty I had acquiring a U.S. work permit. E. F. Hutton told me they would get this matter cleared up while I started to work. So I went to New York and met an immigration lawyer, whom E. F. Hutton paid $3,500 to get the problem settled for me. In the end, after trying all avenues, I couldn't legally get my papers. I was certainly tempted to go a rather dubious route to get the necessary documentation, but I knew I couldn't live with myself. The community in Birmingham found out about my predicament and got behind me. There were newspaper articles written and thousands of signatures gathered on a petition that was sent to an Alabama senator. Despite all these efforts, the bottom line was that I couldn't work legally in the United States.

Now I was in something of a dilemma. I couldn't work in the U.S., but I had one daughter going to university there and the other two in private schools. My most viable option was to return to Canada, so I came back to Toronto and looked at several options, including the Leafs' broadcasting job, before joining one of the brokerage firms. I had to write the Canadian securities exams and then a certain amount of time had to pass before I could actually start selling. In the meantime I commuted between Toronto and Birmingham while I waited for all the paperwork to clear.

By the time I was ready to return, my family didn't want to go. They were happy in Birmingham, and their happiness was important to me. My wife was very involved in the community and with our church. Eleanor had really blossomed in Alabama. She had become the entertainment chairman at our church and had developed into such a good gourmet cook that she had started working at a local restaurant. Eleanor had all the talent needed. What she lacked a little was self-confidence, but in Birmingham she was able to develop her skills and confidence level. Pretty soon she was no longer Mrs. Paul Henderson; instead I became Eleanor's husband!

When you're playing hockey, your wife tends to be in the background. With all the travel involved in playing the woman becomes the central figure in organizing the family. She usually handles all the problems associated with the kids and manages the household. Suddenly, when your career is over, you say, "I'm back now," but she's been doing everything while you were away. Now she might feel she's being shoved into the background again, which can cause a strain in the marriage.

I was lucky to have a wife who enjoyed hockey. She liked the game and loved going to the rink to watch me play. But I was the one who was in the limelight, not her. Even now when I play old-timer hockey I notice the difference. Recently she came to a game and waited for me when it was over. As soon as I came out, a group of people approached me for autographs. I looked over, and there was Eleanor, standing alone about ten feet away from anybody. Being brought up on a farm, she wanted to be a good wife and mother just as her mom had been. I knew this was satisfying to her, but anyone can get tired of being in the distance all the time. When you're playing, you can easily get wrapped up in your career and start to forget about your wife, who also has desires and needs attention. Now that I'm retired from hockey I try to remember this.

I've always been proud to be a strong family man. Even while I was playing, spending time with my family was important. I would go for a beer or two with the guys, but I'd seldom spend all day at a bar. I enjoyed being close to my family and would rather spend my time with them. So, when they didn't want to move back to Canada, I had to listen.

The only way for me to remain in the United States was to go to school, which meant I'd have to cut into my nest egg to pay foreign student tuition. We also knew that two of our daughters would be getting married in the near future, which would mean more expenses. The biggest decision made, however, was to go into Christian work. I had become a born-again Christian in 1975, and all the members of my family had soon followed suit. So I decided to enter the seminary and get direction from there. At this point I was somewhat nervous about making Christian work my vocation, since the financial remuneration for this type of employment was far from appealing. Nevertheless, I felt this was the way to go no matter how expensive it would be. I knew I wanted to spend my life sharing my faith with others because I could see the positive impact it had on me and my family.

8

A New Way of Life

"You know, Grandpa," I said, "you've had a long life."

"Paul," my maternal grandfather replied, "it's gone just like that." He snapped his fingers. "How old are you?"

"Twenty-eight."

"Those years have gone by just like this, haven't they?" He snapped his fingers again. "Before you know it you'll be 48 and you'll sit around and think how fast it's gone. I won't be around to see it, Paul, but that's how you'll feel." And he snapped his fingers one last time.

His point was clear. Life is short, even when you've lived 92 years. No matter how long you live, life is only a small blip in the scheme of things. Eternity, on the other hand, is forever. The day I turned 48 I thought about what my grandfather had said, and when I snapped my fingers, I knew he was right.

When people ask me what I do today, I'm very happy to tell them that I work with a Christian ministry called Campus Crusade for Christ. I find it very rewarding work and enjoy telling people about the Lord and how they can have a better relationship with Him. As far as I'm concerned, there isn't a better job for me today. Mind you, if anyone had told me years ago I'd be doing this as a career, I would have thought they were crazy. How did

I end up in a Christian ministry? It's the result of a process that began after the high of the 1972 Canada-Russian series and the debilitating low that followed. The years between 1973 and 1975 weren't a very good time for me. I didn't know who I was or where I was going in my life.

For two years I had to deal with an internal struggle and a growing sense of discontentment. Most people would say I had no reason to feel this way since I had almost everything I ever wanted. I was a pro hockey player who made good money, had a super marriage, three great kids, and a nice home, drove a fine car, belonged to a country club, was debt free, and had money in the bank. I lived the dream of scoring the big goal and received all the fame possible from that moment. I was told I would always have a positive place in Canadian sports history. Any athlete strives to attain, to win, and maybe to be unique. Even though I had all this, something was missing. The personal glory just wasn't enough. Although I enjoyed the attention, I knew I was after a greater glory.

When I was striving to achieve goals I had set for my life, my focus was clear. I pursued these ambitions intensely because I thought the attainment of these goals would make me successful and happy. Surely, I told myself, contentment would always come from achievement. But when I hit my targets, my feeling of contentment clouded over. "What does it take to make me happy?" I wondered, and then I started thinking about the great questions: What gives meaning to life? Why am I here? What am I really supposed to do?

I knew it was highly unlikely my hockey career would give me the same level of accomplishment I had experienced in the 1972 series. There would be no more big goals to score and I would have to go back and battle against my Team Canada teammates. The Maple Leafs weren't going to be winners. The team had been decimated by the WHA and I was basically told that my best years were behind me. If I had accomplished so much, why wasn't I being rewarded? The kid from Lucknow had made it, but so had lots of other kids from small Canadian towns. What was so special about me? Did I have enough drive left in me to keep up my usual standard of play? I knew I had the skill and talent, but would I have the same level of desire as in the past? Somehow I would have to find the answers because I knew I still wanted to play hockey for a number of years.

Most people in life strive for security. I had no reason to feel anxious about my future. People often told me I was one of the luckiest guys alive. I knew this was true, but when I was honest with myself, I discovered I was far from content. I started asking people some of the questions rolling around in my head, thinking those who were a success should know the answers. This investigation proved fruitless. They weren't able to give me any answers, either. In fact, many of them were equally dissatisfied. Those with the most money seemed to be messed up the worst. Many times their interpersonal relationships were horrific, and in a lot of cases their kids were disasters. Of course, I wasn't perfect, either. When I looked at myself and was truly honest, I saw a prideful, discontented individual. I was less than sensitive with some people and they started to notice and make comments.

During a Florida vacation with some Maple Leaf teammates and their wives, I had a major confrontation with Brian Glennie's then wife, Barbara. Quite frankly she told me I thought too highly of myself and that I tended to be quite arrogant. When I wasn't in a good mood, I could be quite difficult. I always had a rationalization, but there was no excuse. Others on the trip, including the Sittlers and Ellises, were generally in agreement with her observations. She might not have been my favourite person at the time, but I have to admit she made some good points.

At the time people were pulling at me from all directions and invading my territory when I wanted privacy. There were times when I would go along with them and get all dressed up to play the required part. Other times I would get surly. At night, during quieter moments, I didn't feel good about myself. I began to see myself as a hypocrite and was uncomfortable with the person I was becoming. I had time for people whom I needed or could help me, but I think I started to look down on others, and that isn't a good feeling to someone who knows better. For the first time in my life I became very introspective. It was obvious to me that I needed to correct my behaviour. But how would I go about such changes?

Since childhood I had given some thought to religion, having grown up going to the United Church which, of course, was a socially acceptable thing to do. I believed in God and on occasion I would pray, but none of it made any difference in how I lived my life. For an hour every Sunday I would sit in church, but as soon as the service was over, I'd be my own god again. I lived my life as I pleased. The spiritual side of life wasn't in the picture; it was nonexistent. When I started to look at religion more seriously, I went and spoke to a pastor, but he, too, couldn't satisfy the void that had opened up before me. Strangely enough, the person who helped me get some answers was a gentleman named Mel Stevens.

I first met Mel while playing for the Maple Leafs. The operator of a Christian teen ranch in Orangeville, Ontario, Mel gave all the Leaf players beautiful leather-bound Bibles. He decided to do this even though Harold Ballard didn't approve. Ballard eventually banned Mel from the building and even went as far as not letting players leave game tickets for him. None of this discouraged Stevens. He wanted to talk to us no matter what we might have thought of him. Some of the players, myself included, would make fun of the Bibles Mel left for us, even though he went to the trouble to have them inscribed with our names and the Leaf logo. It was a nice personal touch, and I think all the players took the Bibles home.

As I struggled through this restless period in my life, I began to pick up the Bible and read it. At first I found it difficult to understand and certain sections really disturbed me. A little while later Mel came around to my house to ask if I would participate as an instructor at a hockey school he was running at the teen ranch. He wanted me to donate my time, which led me to think he didn't know who I was. For even a week of my time I could have charged a substantial fee. Then he mentioned he was the man who had left Bibles for the Leaf players. "I've been meaning to write you a thank-you note," I told him. "I'm reading the Bible and I have some serious concerns." He offered to help and started asking me questions. Then he encouraged me to look at how I could develop the spiritual side of my life. He also wanted me to think about Christianity. So I set out to read the Bible extensively and study it closely. Mel spoke of eternity and everlasting life. If it was possible to have spiritual life after physical death, I felt I should take the time to examine the matter carefully.

Initially I wasn't sure Christianity was the answer for me. I spent hours reading a great deal of religious literature. Next I looked at several religious movements, then studied for a few months with the Jehovah's Witnesses before deciding I couldn't accept their teaching or interpretation of the scriptures. There seemed to be many possibilities that contained the truth. I had a responsibility to my wife and children and had to look seriously at what I believed and why, since I would have to communicate my feelings to my family.

Because I was full of uncertainties, my investigation was quite thorough. I needed answers to various questions. Is there a God? I wondered. And just who is Jesus Christ? Mel Stevens recommended some excellent books to read along with the Bible. They included *Mere Christianity* by C. S. Lewis, an Oxford University professor, and Josh McDowell's *Evidence That Demands a Verdict*. Both of these authors had been atheists before becoming Christians.

I would then get together with Mel and grill him with more questions. I had so many questions that I nearly drove Mel around the bend. Actually, though, he enjoyed my interrogations because it forced him to study the scriptures at length and to understand the Bible in a deeper way than ever before. I wanted to know why we should accept the Bible readily. It seemed to be a bunch of stories that people interpreted in controversial ways. Was this book reliable? How did it come together? These doubts made my research an excellent exercise. To this day I'm still a student of the Bible.

As I spent this time examining and studying the Bible, I came to learn that Christianity isn't so much a religion as a relationship with God. There is a personal and intimate connection with the Lord when you walk with Him. I reached a point where I wanted to become a Christian. I came to believe there was a God who loved me. I wasn't experiencing His love at this point and I was separated from Him because of the way I lived my life. It wasn't that I was a really bad person, but I had basically lived a life where I went my way and let the Lord go his. Mel

Stevens showed me from the Bible what the consequences were for this separation from God. In His tremendous love for us God sent us His only Son, even though we did nothing to deserve this. Jesus Christ came to Earth, lived a perfect life, and then died on the cross for us. He was buried and rose again. He defeated death and the power of sin over us. We have the opportunity of either accepting or rejecting His love. You accept His love by asking Him to forgive you for the things you've done wrong and then inviting Jesus into your life as your Lord and Saviour.

I understood all of this, but I lacked the courage necessary to make a commitment to become a Christian. I had three reasons for my indecision. First, I was worried about ridicule. What were people going to say? What would the hockey players and the people I golfed with say? I worried about what their reaction might be. Second, I knew I would have to change some things I was doing. I really liked to drink, often too much. My language was atrocious. These habits and others would have to go. Would my life become too narrow? I had always been one of the boys. Lastly, and this was the real clincher, I knew if I loved the Lord, I would have to stand up for Him. The Bible says if we're ashamed of Him, He will be ashamed of us. I would have to stand up and be counted if I really meant it. To me this was very intimidating. There is no way I'll ever feel comfortable with this, I thought to myself. This internal debate went on for several months.

One day in March 1975 I was alone at home. I had spoken to God on many occasions just as I would talk to anyone, and on this particular day I remember telling Him I was petrified. I said to God, "I believe you are who you say you are. I can't even comprehend why you would love me and why you love me enough to send your only Son to die for me, but I accept your love. I want to have eternal life and I believe in you with all my heart. I want to have a relationship with you. I ask you to forgive me for all the things I have ever done. Here is my life. It's yours. You make me the person you want me to be." Before I ended my conversation with the Lord I added, "Now don't expect me to go out and tell anybody about this! I know I'll never have the courage to do it."

Finally, though, I made the commitment to become a Christian. I didn't feel any different other than knowing the struggle was over and I had surrendered. However, I had no intention of telling anyone. I was so scared! Of course, I knew I would have to say something to my family eventually, but it took me three or four days to work up enough courage to tell Eleanor. She's my best friend in the whole world, and I should have been able to tell her anything. We were at the kitchen table when I decided to tell her. My mouth went dry and my heart started to pound. I think Eleanor thought I was having a heart attack or something. She was very understanding about how difficult my struggle had been for me, but at this point she wanted no part of my decision for herself. It took me another week before I told Mel Stevens I had stepped over the line and had invited the Lord into my life. As time passed, I got to the point where I wanted to tell people because I realized the difference God made in my life. In fact, I probably got a little too aggressive in the early days of my new life.

At first Eleanor wasn't too excited about me becoming a Christian. She was cool to the whole idea. She saw herself as a good person who attended church on Sunday. Religion, to her, was nothing to get excited about. Our difference of opinion caused a strain in our marriage for a while. But Mel Stevens was smart enough to tell me not to preach to her. He told me to love her as I always had, to be a good husband, and let her find her space. In the next little while Eleanor said she noticed a considerable change in me. I had always been the type who could never sit still. I constantly had to have something on the go. Eleanor now saw a quietness and contentment in me and knew I was a different person on the inside. I was able to relax and was generally much calmer. She decided there must be something to this, so she started asking questions, and when she did, she became more receptive. She found out she wasn't as good as she thought, and three months later came to understand the need to have the Saviour in her life. Ultimately our three daughters all prayed and asked Jesus to be their Saviour and Lord also.

The reaction of friends was interesting. I spoke to many of them on an individual basis. Some of them wanted to hear what I had to say, others didn't. Many, like me, were afraid to look for answers to some vital questions because they knew they might have to do something about it. If they wanted to know more, I would try to give them direction, but usually I steered them to Mel Stevens. I introduced Mel to many Leaf players, and he had a dramatic effect on the lives of Ron Ellis, Darryl Sittler, and Laurie Boschman. I don't try to push people because I remember it took me a long time to cross over the line, but I'm always available to those who are searching. Some of my best friends today are people whom I shared the gospel with and who are now Christians.

Often, for people to become receptive about God or Christianity, something dramatic must happen in their lives. Frequently it's not a positive event. The death of a child, the end of a marriage, or financial ruin will cause people to stop and consider where their lives are going.

Ironically enough, in my case it was just the opposite. I had everything I wanted. If I wanted something bigger or better, I knew I could get it. I was at my peak, but when I climbed the mountain and looked around, I thought, Is this all there is to life? At that point I became teachable, willing to listen and learn. When people open themselves up, they can find the answers if they're willing to persevere.

It's easy to understand why people might be sceptical about religion. To some, religion was a ritual that was shoved down their throats, something they had to do. It wasn't always a pleasant experience. Like me, they saw Christianity as a bunch of do's and don'ts. They were naturally attracted to the don'ts. No one taught them to love God, only to fear Him. This is tragic. Others are turned off by poor leadership. Financial and sexual scandals have involved people with high profiles in the religious community. Some Christians have difficulty dealing with success and they fall into bad situations. I'm often reminded of a saying, which states that for every 999 people who can deal with adversity, only one can handle success. We have a tendency to look at bad examples, which isn't a good thing to do. There is only one person we should ever look at and that is the Lord himself. I'm mindful not to be judgemental. The Bibles tells us not to judge anyone. Christians are as human as anyone. We all have feet of clay and we all need a Saviour. Fortunately God is forgiving and faithful even when we aren't.

The best thing about Christianity is that God accepts you right where you are. I don't have to compare myself with anyone else. There's no competition. I can just be Paul Henderson. You develop a relationship with Christ that isn't a bunch of do's and don'ts. If you love the Lord, there will be some indication of this in your life. For me, it's a need to spend time alone with the Lord every day, and I really desire to make my life count in a positive way for the Lord. But many days I disappoint even myself and realize how thankful I am that I've been saved by God's grace through faith and that I don't have to earn it, since it is the greatest gift ever given by God.

I used to think people involved in religion were basically weak individuals who needed a crutch. I saw them as people who couldn't handle their problems, so they got the Lord involved. Or they were people who could do nothing else with their lives. If you couldn't make it in the world, go join the Christians. They'll take anyone. In his book Darryl Sittler told of the moment he was on the ice after he scored the winning goal in the 1976 Canada Cup. He turned to Gerry Cheevers and said, "Maybe now I can become a born-again Christian like Paul Henderson!" Darryl wrote that it was a cheap shot. If Darryl hadn't become a Christian, he would never have felt this way. I know because I used to do the same thing. In large part this was due to an ingrained attitude in professional hockey towards those who are Christians. Today I believe Christians are some of the strongest people I know as well as excellent athletes.

It's easy to illustrate this point. I could name top players in every professional sport who are Christians. For example, in hockey there are players like Ryan Walter (978 career games played, 231 goals, 643 points, 936 penalty minutes), Mike Gartner (1,005 games played, 538 goals, 1,039 points, 918 penalty minutes), Laurie Boschman (939 games played, 220 goals, 553 points, 2,164 penalty minutes), and Mark Osborne (733 games played, 190 goals, 287 assists, 477 points, 899 penalty minutes), just to name a few, who are devout Christians. It doesn't interfere with their jobs. All these players have had long careers, and they've never shied away from the rough stuff. A Christian is as dedicated as any athlete. He comes to play because he knows he has a responsibility to the Lord to be in good shape and to perform to the best of his ability. Just because you become a Christian, doesn't mean your personality changes on the ice. If you're an aggressive guy like Boschman, you'll continue to be that way. If you're a skilled player like Mike Gartner, you'll play the game that way.

It also can't be said that Christians aren't leaders or motivators. The 1991 Grey Cup game coaches Adam Rita (Toronto) and Wally Buono (Calgary) are both strong Christians. Joe Gibbs, a three-time Super Bowl winner with the Washington Redskins, is a Christian, so is another very successful NFL coach, Dan Reeves with Denver. Or how about Lou Holtz at Notre Dame, or the legendary Tom Landry, who coached the Dallas Cowboys for 29 years? Do these coaches get their teams to play tough, aggressive, winning football? You bet they do. On-field Christian leaders include quarterbacks Damon Allen (now with Hamilton), Danny Barrett (Vancouver), Kent Austin (Saskatchewan and Grey Cup MVP in 1989), and Toronto Argonauts Reggie Pleasant, Carl Brazley, and Pinball Clemons, the latter the CFL MVP in 1990.

If you want to look at baseball, you don't have to go any farther than Joe Carter of the Toronto Blue Jays and five of his teammates. Carter has played a large role in the Jays' success, as did Greg Gagne for the Minnesota Twins when they were champions in 1987 and 1991. Orel Herschiser (World Series MVP in 1988) and Darryl Strawberry (a very new Christian) are both vital to the chances of the Los Angeles Dodgers. All these Christian players are successful as team players and champions.

Not everybody reacts well to Christian athletes, at least not at first. When I was in the WHA, there was a tough defenceman named Bill Butters who played with New England, Minnesota, Houston, and Edmonton. He moved around a lot but always managed to get well over 100 minutes in penalties by the time the season was finished. This guy was an animal, and the stories about him are incredible.

Butters took delight in riding me about being a Christian. "Watch out for Henderson. He'll hit you with a Bible!" he'd say loud enough for everybody to hear. The fans would laugh. I hated the guy. I would think good Christian thoughts like, I hope he steps out on the ice and breaks his leg. I was always thrilled when Butters was out of the lineup when we were playing against his team. I would have been happy to see him out of the league just to avoid his taunts.

I wasn't that lucky, however. One night the Birmingham Bulls were playing against Butters and his team. During the warm-up before the game, as I was skating behind our net, I looked up and saw Butters motioning to me from centre ice. Obviously a confrontation was imminent. I turned to my right, and who do I see, but teammate Gilles Bilodeau, whose main ambition as a hockey player was to get 500 minutes in penalties for one season! "Gilles," I said, "there's going to be trouble at centre ice."

"Terrific! Let's go!" he yelled without any hesitation.

I skated to centre ice, not sure what was going to happen next. When we got close to each other, Butters looked me straight in the eye and asked, "Paul, do you have any information about that Christianity stuff of yours?"

"What?" I blurted out, not believing my ears, "Are you serious?"

"I've never been more serious in my life," Butters replied.

To make a long story short, several months later Bill

prayed to receive the Lord. Today he's involved with Hockey Ministries International and lives in Minnesota. Bill might have been as far away from the Lord as anyone, but even he came to realize he needed the Saviour in his life.

Generally speaking, Christian players don't cause trouble or turmoil, but it isn't realistic to expect them to be perfect because of their religious beliefs. They can get ticked off and upset just as much as the next person. They go through bad times athletically in the game as another ball player might. When things do go wrong, people tend to point to Christianity as being somehow at fault. Having your Christian faith ridiculed because of your performance, especially by the media, is something you learn to deal with. As I said before, I've received good treatment from the press, including the time after I became a Christian. Frank Orr, in particular, wrote an excellent article about my newfound Christianity. I appreciated that very much and wrote him a thank-you letter.

Both baseball and football have opened their doors and accepted Christian athletes. Players are allowed to organize in prayer, and people from the Christian community are invited to speak to athletes. In hockey it's not nearly so open, but things are improving. Role models like Ryan Walter are showing the way for other Christian hockey players. Even former coach and *Hockey Night in Canada* commentator Don Cherry defends Christian hockey players. It's well-known that Don likes rough, tough players. To his credit he has no trouble sticking up for Christians. Cherry knows that religion has nothing to do with how a man plays the game.

After my hockey career was over and a couple of opportunities didn't work out, I decided to make Christianity my life's work. I felt God was urging me to make this decision. I wish I could say I was excited about the choice, but I wasn't. I felt I was making a tremendous sacrifice and only obeyed because of my faith in Him. Since I could only stay in the United States as a student, I entered a seminary in Birmingham. There I studied and took courses that prepared me for what I do today. I have no plans to become an ordained minister, however. I made a decision not to become a minister or pastor with my own church, since I don't think it would be an appropriate or effective platform for me.

By 1984 I was still unable to get my work papers, so I decided to leave the United States and return to Canada. I had wanted to stay in the States in part to prove to myself that I could make it out in the world without being Paul Henderson the hockey player. Ego is a tough thing to deal with, even for a Christian. As I thought about it more, I realized I had a natural platform that few others have, so why waste it? Canada was the place the Lord could use me most. I wanted to open as many doors as possible, and I could only hope to achieve this in Canada by basing myself in the Toronto area.

Many people will meet with me today because they want me to talk about the 1972 series or to converse with a former hockey player. At the right moment, if the opportunity presents itself, I'll speak to the person about the spiritual side of life. It it's not appropriate, then I won't bring the subject up at all. I've found that people are less intimidated talking to an ex-hockey player about spiritual issues than they might be with a pastor or priest. I'm glad we returned to Canada which, to me, is the best country in the world.

Currently I work for a Christian ministry called Campus Crusade for Christ, which is made up of 14 different ministries, two of which I'm involved in. The first is Ath-

letes in Action, a division devoted to working with athletes. Although I started by working in this area, I'm less
active today. I found I like working with the Leadership
Ministries division, which is dedicated to working with
business executives and professionals. My ministry works
specifically with businessmen to help them develop their
relationships with the Lord. These men are successful in
the business world, but I try to help them develop their
spiritual life, particularly their relationships with the
Lord. I encourage these men to think about how they as
businessmen, husbands, and fathers can make their lives
count for the Lord. Pushing men out of their comfort
zones in asking some of the questions I once tried to re-
solve is a big part of my role at the ministry. We also try
to teach them how to pray, to be students of the Bible, to
memorize scripture and, when appropriate, to share their
faith with others. I tell them my story and let them know
what the Lord has done for me. It's not a question of jam-
ming anything down someone's throat. We approach
from the point of view of opening a person's mind and
attempt to get him or her to investigate further. If they
choose to pursue matters, then I'm available for them.

We work in groups and also in one-on-one counselling
sessions. I give talks in churches and at outreach events.
My work takes me all over Canada, with enough requests
to keep me busier than I want to be many times. There's
no shortage of demand for what we do, and we'll deal
with anyone who seeks our assistance. They could be
Catholic, Anglican, Lutheran, Presbyterian, Jewish, agnos-
tic, or atheist. It doesn't matter. We aren't a replacement
for the church, and we strongly urge people to go to a
religious institution of their choice. We respect all faiths at
our ministry.

My belief is that the Lord wanted me in a ministry

where I could reach out and help men in particular. I think my ministry is having an impact. I've helped many to come to know the Lord. It's wonderful to see men grow and develop and witness the tremendous influence Christianity has on their lives as businessmen, husbands, and fathers. I've learned to appreciate my relationships with other men. Today I know there are men out there who care about what happens to me. I can call on them anywhere, anytime. I could be in some remote part of the world and still know there was a good friend at the other end of the line. I notice I've become a much better listener. I think this comes with appreciating the value of a good friendship.

I've tried to teach businessmen more about the Bible. I tell them there's a great deal of business advice to be found there. The scriptures can help you to organize and run a company. I talked to one man who said he spent thousands of dollars putting letters behind his name with all his degrees. After being involved with our ministry for six months, he told me he found more information and knowledge in the Bible than he had ever imagined. He found the Book of Proverbs to be an excellent manual for running a business. People can make light of the Bible, but those of us who have taken the time to read it see much in the Good Book that is applicable and relevant in today's world.

Darryl Sittler wrote in his autobiography about how he tends to be much more private about his Christianity, while Paul Henderson wants to tell everyone about it. I laughed a little and thought, Oh, if it were only true. There are too many times that I don't take advantage of a good situation. I look at it this way, if I found a cure for cancer, I certainly wouldn't keep quiet about it. To me, accepting the Lord into my life was the greatest thing ever to happen to me. How could I possibly keep quiet about that? I think some people are called to lead and take a stand. The Lord wants me to go out and tell people about what I believe. This isn't something everyone is comfortable doing. My wife is a lot like Darryl. If someone wants to know about her experiences, she will talk to them, but she isn't nearly as aggressive as I am when an opportunity presents itself. I'm glad I have the chance to speak to thousands of people every year through the ministry.

I wish I could say that becoming a Christian will make a person's life a bed of roses but, in fact, I can attest to the fact that there is no such promise from the Lord. I spent the worst night of my life as a Christian. In 1983, while living in Birmingham, Eleanor needed some surgery done. It went well, but complications developed. I was in the room at 1:00 a.m. as three doctors worked on her. The doctor who had performed the surgery was a friend of ours, and I could see how heavily he was perspiring. Things didn't look good at all. I went over to Eleanor and lifted her hand. "Honey," she said to me, "I don't know if I can make it." I could feel my stomach lurch, and I had to step into the hall just outside the room.

Upset and in tears, I shook my fist at the Lord and said, "Don't you take her from me!" I'd given everything to the Lord except for Eleanor. It took me a long time to give myself to the Lord, even longer to turn my finances over to Him and finally give Him my children. But I had never given Him my wife. She was the most precious thing I had on earth. I would have done anything, paid any price to save her. As I was going through these emotions, I came to the realization that the situation was out of my hands. I couldn't play *Let's Make a Deal* with the Lord. He doesn't work that way. Then a quietness came over me. I stopped crying and said to the Lord, "Even if you take her, I'll still walk with you. I don't know how I'll make it and I'll be totally heartbroken, but you've proven yourself to me."

Composed, I went back into the room, took Eleanor's hand, and told her, "You fight this!" She pulled through, and I survived the worst night of my life with the help of the Lord.

I get a real kick watching my young grandson Josh, who talks to the Lord as if He were his best friend. Once I asked Josh to give the blessing before a meal at a golf tournament I had organized for businessmen. There were close to 150 men in the room, and Josh said the blessing without any problem. Nothing makes me happier than to see my grandson walk with the Lord.

Long before I retired from hockey I told Eleanor I would never get a job in the sport when it came time to hang up my skates. Ironically I have Harold Ballard to thank for keeping that promise. If he had allowed me to do the radio broadcasts of Leaf games, who knows what direction my life might have taken? I actually wrote Ballard a letter, thanking him and explaining how my life had changed. He never replied. He was probably as surprised as I was to know I was involved in Christian work.

Perhaps people like Ballard have the wrong idea about what is meant by the term "born-again Christian." When I first heard it, I thought it meant you were a Christian at one point and had turned away, or something similar, but that isn't the case. Everyone is born physically and one day they will die. The Bible says we are born into sin and we are spiritually dead. God then gives us the opportunity, the choice, to be born spiritually. There is no particular age when this should happen. At some point when you hear the Gospel you have the choice of accepting Jesus Christ or rejecting him. When you accept Jesus Christ into your life, you're telling the Lord you understand. You ask him to wipe the slate clean and recognize that you need a Lord and Saviour. In giving your life to the Lord you become a Christian. At that moment in time, as you were once born physically, you are now born spiritually, hence the phrase "born again." It's kind of like saying "I do" when you get married. When you say "I do," your intentions are clear. As a Christian, you understand the facts about what your commitment to the Lord means.

A wise Christian once said that we should plan each day as if we'll live forever and live each day as if it's our last. I try to make every day count, especially by trying to help others wherever they are at this point in their journey.

Today I wouldn't change places with anyone. I have no plans to retire until I'm 75 years old. Maybe then I'll slow down to just three or four days a week. I enjoy this work so much I intend to do it as long as the Lord wants me to. Perhaps one day I'll be doing something different in a new country. When you live by your faith in the Lord and your willingness to walk with Him, you take life one day at a time.

9

The Goal

Here's a shot! Henderson made a wild stab for it and
fell. Here's another shot, right in front. They score!
Henderson has scored for Canada!
> — *Foster Hewitt's play-by-play broadcast*
> *of eighth game, Moscow, September 28, 1972*

Rarely does a day go by when I don't talk about the Goal.
Almost everyone I meet wants to tell me what he or she
was doing when I scored the winning goal in Moscow. I
might discuss the goal between 275 and 300 days in a
year. Since there's no escaping it, I've learned to enjoy all
the tidbits people throw my way with their recollections
of the event. The more time passes, the more I appreciate
the moment.

Between 1976 and 1984 I lived in the United States.
When I returned to Canada, I figured the fans would
have forgotten about me, but I couldn't have been more
wrong. Even today, no matter where I go, Canadians
want to thank me for scoring the goal. This can happen to
me anywhere. For instance, just recently I went to meet a
friend at the airport. In the short time I waited for him to
come out of the arrival gate at least five people came over
and introduced themselves. Naturally they started to talk
about the goal. As others passed by, I heard them whisper, "There's Paul Henderson."

People from the U.S. who know me are amazed to see
the reaction I get. A friend from Birmingham stayed over
with us for a few days after he helped me move back to

Canada in 1984. We were out for dinner one night when people in the restaurant came over and asked for autographs. My friends knew I had been away for a long time and couldn't believe people were still interested in an event that happened in 1972. It surprised me, too, and is perhaps indicative of what hockey means to Canadians.

The person who probably gets the greatest kick out of the recognition the goal brings is my grandson Josh. He was born in 1983, but he knows all about the goal and has a picture of it in his room. Josh loves when people ask me for my autograph. He stays with us for part of the summer holidays. If we're out and people approach him, he's quick to tell his grandmother, "They wanted Grampy's autograph and they wanted to talk about the Goal." He seems to relish the whole thing.

Currently I travel all over Canada. From east to west I usually get the same reaction. Sometimes I think everyone in Canada is a hockey fan. I find the exception now is if someone *doesn't* talk to me about the goal. I never tire of it because the stories are all different and always interesting. Now that I'm used to it, I find listening to these anecdotes a pleasurable experience. The stories are happy, funny, often quite touching, and say a great deal about the human spirit. It's a marvellous feeling to be remembered for such an uplifting moment.

Here are a few of the many stories I've collected over the years.

A lady once wrote me a letter, telling me I owed her some money. She and her husband had just moved into a new home. She was unpacking some dishes and setting them down on a table while the game played on the television. At the moment I scored the goal she had a dish in each hand. She lost control for a few seconds and threw the dishes into the air. The fine china went straight up, hit the ceiling, fell back, and shattered into a thousand pieces. She said she didn't know whether to shout for joy or cry. She wrote that the goal was one of the greatest thrills in her life. I think she might have been a little embarrassed to tell her husband how the dishes had been broken. Maybe her insurance company looked after her loss!

• • •

A gentleman in Ontario wrote me a letter, wanting me to compensate him for his lost tackle box and fishing gear. He and two of his friends were out fishing in a small boat. They had the game on the radio. When I scored the goal, he jumped up and got so excited that he went overboard. When he fell into the water, he must have knocked his tackle box flying over the side of the boat. The tackle box was full of stuff he needed for fishing. He was saved, but he lost the box for good. Since he felt I was responsible, he thought it would be a good idea if I helped him replace the lost equipment. Good luck!

• • •

People like to show me damage caused in their home because of the goal. Chairs and desks have been the main items dented with a few chandeliers thrown in for good measure. I remember one man showing me his desk with a big gouge in it. "When you scored the goal," he told me, "I threw my chair back and it smashed the desk. I won't fix it because it will always remind me of the goal." Another man kept a broken chair as a "souvenir" of the goal. It's still in his recreation room just as it was in September 1972. People have also shown me stains on the walls from the beer they were drinking, which splattered when they leaped in celebration. They can point to the exact spot. It's strange what people consider a memento!

•••

One of the best letters I received was from a woman in Toronto who told me about how her marriage was saved by the goal. This lady and her husband had recently separated. They had decided they were going to get a divorce. On the day of the final game he came over to the house to pick up a few items. When he got there, the third period was about to start. He noticed she had the game on and asked if he could sit down and watch the end. So they sat there and watched the game without saying a word to each other.

When I scored the goal, they both jumped up, started dancing, and hugged each other. As they embraced, they looked into each other's eyes and realized they were still in love. It was an emotional moment for them. With a new perspective they decided to move back in together. She wrote to me around Christmas about three months after the goal and said that I had given her the most wonderful Christmas gift ever because her marriage had been saved. They had worked their differences out. If I hadn't scored, he might have left without looking at her again. A letter like that gives you a warm feeling inside.

•••

One day, after speaking at a church, two grizzled farmers introduced themselves to me. They wanted to tell me how they had celebrated the goal. On a farm just north of Toronto they were doing some work in a silo and listening to the game on a radio. When I scored, they grabbed each other, started dancing, and shouted with delight. The silo echoed their shouts, but they kept on dancing with each other. The one who told me this story laughed so hard while he was talking that tears sprang from his eyes. "I'm glad nobody saw us dancing like two old fools," he told me. "They would have locked us up for good."

• • •

A funny situation developed at a teachers' convention in Toronto while the final game was being played. A guest speaker from the United States was giving a speech to the assembly but didn't know that a lot of people in the audience were listening to the game on their transistor radios. When Yvan Cournoyer scored to make it 5-5, there was a slight reaction among the people listening. The speaker, who had no idea what was going on regarding the game, was startled for a moment, but then continued his talk.

When I scored, the place went wild, which astonished the speaker. He couldn't understand what was going on. He was fairly certain this reaction wasn't caused by something he had said. It must have seemed as if the crowd had gone temporarily insane. Finally someone let him in on what had happened. I wonder if he saw the humour in it all.

• • •

In Listowel, Ontario, they used to have an annual ploughing match. In 1972 it was held on the day of the eighth game in Moscow. Many attending the event brought a radio along to listen to the game. As one farmer was setting out to plough a field, he placed a radio on top of his tractor. The key to doing well in the contest was to maintain a straight line and plough the rows accordingly.

When he was about three-quarters of the way down the field, I scored the goal. He leaped onto the hood of the tractor and started dancing while the machine was still running. Then he looked back and saw that his rows were hardly straight. He had swerved all over the place. He didn't win the match, but at least we made him happy by winning the game!

• • •

Three men were travelling in a car on the Trans-Canada Highway in a very remote part of the Northwest Territories. Their radio reception was poor because they were driving in an area of peaks and valleys. When the car crested a hill with about five minutes to play in the game, they decided to pull over and listen to the final moments. In that cold land people rarely pulled over unless they had a serious problem. Normally you wanted to keep the car moving so you could operate the heater at maximum warmth. But they had to listen to the conclusion.

When I scored the goal, they jumped out of the car, ran around, and shouted like wildmen. "We won! We won!" they screamed. As they were doing this, another car came by and noticed these men off to the side of the road. The people in this new vehicle had no idea what was going on. In the middle of the Arctic they probably expected not to meet many people on such a lonely road. Yet here in one of the farthest northern points in Canada they came across three men, yelling and screaming in the freezing cold. They had to pull over and investigate. When they got the explanation, they were somewhat relieved. Originally they had assumed these men had gone mad. They must have thought the cold had done them in, but I think the result warmed all their hearts.

• • •

A disc jockey from Toronto told me the next story. He went a little crazy on the air when I scored the winning goal in the final game Thursday afternoon. The next day, Friday, he was a DJ at a dance. About halfway through the affair he announced that he would play "O Canada" to celebrate the victory the day before. He told me there wasn't a dry eye in the place as the anthem played. People sang the lyrics while their eyes filled with tears of joy. Even the DJ said he was blubbering. Obviously the emotions were still flowing strong a day later.

• • •

Some people were on a Canadian air flight during the final game. The pilot provided updates for the passengers. He came on the PA system and told everyone we were down 5-3 at the end of two. Next he gave them the news when we made it 5-4 and then 5-5. When it was over, the pilot announced we had won the game 6-5. The passengers and crew spontaneously broke out into "O Canada." Everyone was so happy that the crew decided to give the passengers an extra free drink! Maybe these people owe me a few on the house.

• • •

Because the last game was played on a Thursday afternoon I get many stories from people who were in school on September 28, 1972. One man in Toronto, now in his thirties, told me how his teacher kept him from watching the game. "Our teacher made us stay in class and we didn't get to see the game," he said. "I've hated that teacher ever since." Watching him tell me the story, I could see that his animosity towards the teacher was real. He is as upset about the incident today as he was when it happened. I hope his telling me this story will make him feel better. To all the teachers who let their students watch the game, you did the right thing!

• • •

In another instance a man told me a story about how he and three others in law school at Queen's University were supposed to write their bar exam on Friday, the day after the final game. They normally would have been studying to make their final preparations for what might be the most important test of their lives. Instead they watched the game! "We had to watch it," he told me. "There was no way we were going to miss it." They watched the game and then spent about two hours coming down from the high they had experienced. After that they studied all night and passed their exams the next day. Maybe Team Canada's win inspired them.

• • •

A doctor form Oakville, Ontario, told me his story a little while ago. In 1972 he was working at a clinic in Mississauga. On the day of the final game he told me his patients got some of the quickest medical attention in history. Every so often he would sneak out to the pharmacy next door where they had a small black-and-white TV. He would catch a glimpse of the game and then head back to his office for his next patient. With about five minutes to go he told his receptionist, "I'm not seeing anybody else until the game's over. You'll have to tell them to wait."

He went back to the pharmacy where a crowd had now gathered for the last moments of the series. Everything and everybody seemed to stop. He said the group of people in the pharmacy started to cheer, "We want Henderson! We want Henderson!" They wanted coach Harry Sinden to put me on. When I jumped into the play and scored the goal, they yelled, "We told you! We told you!"

• • •

Women have told me perhaps the strangest stories regarding the goal. About five women have said they actually prayed I would score the winning goal. No man has ever told me anything like this. I have never prayed to God to let me score a goal or to win any particular game, including the time after I became a born-again Christian. It would make me uncomfortable to pray such a prayer. I can only recall asking the Lord to help me give it my best. I honestly have no idea why these women were praying for me specifically to score the goal. Maybe it was due to the fact I had scored the two previous winning goals. I didn't know what to make of that, but after I became a Christian I thought about those game-winning goals a whole lot more. There could be more to them than meets the eye, but I won't know for sure this side of heaven.

• • •

One Catholic lady was so desperate that she promised the Lord she would go to church every day for a month if I scored. She said she started well but didn't make it and hoped the Lord would understand. Another woman told me she was never much of a hockey fan and hadn't watched the game in years but was totally immersed in the last three matches in Moscow. As time flashed by in the final period, she found herself praying for me, which was also rather unusual for her. She said she just felt compelled to do so and remembers thanking the Lord when I scored.

• • •

A mother told me a story about her son playing road hockey just after I scored the goal. In the excitement of the afternoon some young boys decided they wanted to play a game right away. The problems began when all the boys wanted to be Paul Henderson. "I'm Paul Henderson! I'm Paul Henderson!" they cried. The mother of this little guy had to go out and try to settle the dispute. Later this same kid had his mother go out and get a "Paul Henderson helmet." No ordinary helmet would do. I had started doing promotions with CCM for hockey equipment, so this new interest in helmets worked out quite nicely for me. At the time not many NHL players were wearing helmets. Maybe this kid was one of the first to emulate a player with a helmet!

• • •

The final game became an international event for one family. A young man found himself in England during the series. Before the last match he telephoned Canada and spoke to his father. "Now, Dad," he said, "you be sure and phone me as soon as the game is over and let me know who won." The father agreed to do so.

As soon as I scored the goal, the father grabbed the telephone and called his son overseas. "We won, we won!" he yelled into the handset. He was so out of control and talking so loudly that the son couldn't understand a word.

"Dad, settle down. Who scored? Who won the game?"

The father just repeated, "We won, we won, we beat the Russians!"

The son didn't find out until later what the commotion was all about. He thought his father had lost his mind there for a while!

• • •

One of the most heartwarming aspects of scoring the goal was how it brought people together. A woman told me a story of how the goal reunited her family, which was on the verge of a breakup because of a deep rift between her husband and son. The boy was 14 at the time and had stopped talking to his father for several months.

Somehow the father and son watched the final game from Moscow together. After I put the puck past Tretiak, they sprang to their feet and cheered. In their exuberance they found themselves hugging each other. The touching and holding seemed to break the barrier between them, and the strain in their relationship disappeared instantly.

As the dinner hour approached, they were still excited by what had happened. While they ate their meal that night, they looked at everything from a different angle. For the father, the boy who couldn't do anything right now seemed like his son again.

"You absolutely changed the whole atmosphere in my family," the woman told me. "I was caught in the middle between those two. I'll be eternally grateful."

• • •

My final story involves my own daughters, Heather and Jennifer. They went to the same public school and watched the game separately with their classmates. Heather was standing on a table watching the game when I scored the goal. Her classmates charged, and she was knocked backwards onto the floor. They mobbed her until a friend jumped in and offered her protection. The kids were so out of control that they had to dismiss the entire school.

Heather tried to find Jennifer so she could take her home, where Wendy Sittler waited with our other girl, Jill. The Sittlers had moved into our house to look after our daughters while we were away. With some difficulty Heather and Jennifer managed to get home, followed by a bunch of kids.

People started coming to the door, looking for autographs and pictures. So many people came by that the girls put up a sign that read: We Have No Autographs Left. The phone kept ringing so much that they finally had to take the telephone receiver off the hook. Wendy didn't know what to do when somebody started to nail a sign on the deck above our bedroom, and I'm sure she was glad when Darryl got back to help her handle this unexpected attention.

• • •

There can be no doubt that our victory in Moscow brought Canadians together as never before. People united in a totally unplanned and unrehearsed manner. They found themselves doing things they might never have contemplated before the goal was scored. A man told me he was in university in 1972. He watched the game with seven or eight guys. "When you scored," he said, "we started hugging one another. I wouldn't have hugged one of those guys in a hundred years, but you had to share the moment with somebody." People have told me they had to go someplace where others were gathered. If people found themselves alone, they headed to their local bar or to a mall where a television was set up.

There were stories of people streaming out into the streets, stopping traffic and proudly waving the Canadian flag. After three tension-filled hours that ended with a sensational climax to a terrific hockey game and series, Canadians had a great need to demonstrate their love for their country.

People on Yonge Street in Toronto had no trouble showing their emotions. An article in the *Toronto Sun* by Susan Ford, dated September 29, 1972, told of "a man with a trumpet who appeared immediately after the game on the corner of Yonge and Bloor streets and played "O Canada" to the delight and cheers of passersby and office workers who were hanging out of windows and applauding." In 1992 I met the trumpeter with a group of people. He played the anthem again, and the people I was with all stood and sang "O Canada."

Once I thought about what might have happened if I hadn't scored the goal. I had called Peter Mahovlich off the ice. What if the Russians had broken out and scored a goal? What if it had been my man? Remember, they had a great chance to clear the zone while I was down behind the net. What would Canadians have thought of me then? Luckily, though, I scored the goal and photographer Frank Lennon captured the moment with his now-famous photograph.

I get a new story about the goal on an almost daily basis. By now I should have run out of people who watched the game or the memories should have faded, but that hasn't been the case at all. Many of the stories included here are anecdotes I picked up in the past year alone. Obviously the joy of that moment on Thursday, September 28, 1972, still burns bright in the minds of many Canadians.

10

Reflections

ON THE MAPLE LEAFS

I'm a big Cliff Fletcher fan. I played for him in Atlanta and always liked the way he treated me. Cliff is a classy individual who is dedicated to winning and, given time, fans and players will see a difference in the Maple Leafs. With his experience Cliff knows what to do in order to rebuild the team. It won't happen overnight, but we can already see Cliff's influence on the organization. He's hired some very good people to help him, and I have a good feeling about the Leafs' future.

Another positive note about Cliff Fletcher's hiring is that he learned his trade with the Montreal Canadiens, an organization that has been properly run for years, largely due to its continuity in management. They've been able to develop and maintain an aura of winning. To do that you have to understand the value of tradition, something the Canadiens have always fully grasped. When you walk into the Forum, and in particular the Canadiens' dressing room, you can see how the tradition is kept alive with pictures and plaques. The Habs also like to have their former greats around, a fact highlighted by the presence of Jean Beliveau in their front office as a vice president. Players love to associate with winners like Jean. They want to win Stanley Cups the way he did.

For former Leaf players the atmosphere around Maple Leaf Gardens has changed dramatically. I don't think ex-Leafs have ever asked for much. We wanted to be treated with respect and have a chance to participate in various events. In 1990 the Leafs Alumni was established, and we played a game against the Montreal Canadiens Alumni at the Gardens, an event that was quite successful.

As the 1991-92 season began, the Leafs invited some former players to travel by train with the team to Montreal for the season opener as part of the NHL's 75th anniversary celebrations. The occasion brought back memories for me and guys like Ronnie Ellis. During the nostalgic train ride, Ronnie and I laughed about the old days and shared war stories of playing in places like Montreal and Chicago. When we went into the Montreal Forum and the Chicago Stadium the adrenaline would always be flowing. You wanted to play especially well in certain arenas.

It was good to travel with Ronnie Ellis again. He was my closest friend during my hockey career, and the chemistry between us was great not only on the ice but off it, as well. Our wives also got along quite well, which made socializing easy. Today I talk with Ronnie about three or four times a week and we usually find time to play golf. Our personalities are actually quite different. Ronnie is more methodical, detail-oriented, and quiet. I tend to be more spontaneous and outgoing. Opposites can attract in a positive way when the mix is good, and Eleanor and I have always enjoyed the company of Ron and Jan Ellis.

Riding the train brought back memories of team pranks, notably rookie initiations. Having been initiated as a rookie, I enjoyed being part of the ritual as a veteran.

One night on a train returning from Montreal a group of vets decided to shave a rookie or two. I was with Dave Keon, Tim Horton, Ron Ellis, George Armstrong, Floyd Smith, Murray Oliver, and Norm Ullman. We were feeling no pain after polishing off a few beers. However, our gang made a slight miscalculation. There were more rookies around than we could handle. We had to deal with big guys like Jim Dorey, Pat Quinn, Brad Selwood, Mike Pelyk, and Rick Ley, who managed to turn the tables on us! It was lucky for us that we had Tim Horton on our side. He could take on about six guys all by himself. During the scuffle, Tim took an elbow from Pat Quinn in the nose and started bleeding all over the place. Obviously these rookies were too strong for us.

Looking back at the incident now, I think it was hilarious, although today it might appear to be an idiotic way to develop team spirit. The shave isn't used as much nowadays, but the 1990-91 Leafs did eventually initiate Alexander Godynyuk (since traded to Calgary) and Rob Pearson in this manner. No matter what is done, it all goes towards saying, "You're one of us now." After the initiation, the rookie starts to feel part of the team.

The Toronto organization is moving in a direction where the players will soon wear the Maple Leaf with pride. Anyone associated with the Leafs should have plenty of incentive to win if only for their loyal fans. I've talked to Leaf fans all over Canada. Many of them have supported the team since the days of Foster Hewitt's radio broadcasts. They got tired of all the losing and the nonsense that surrounded the once-great organization. However, many remained faithful. Next to my playing in the 1972 Canada-Russia series, I get most recognized as a Maple Leaf. Anywhere I travel in Canada people like to talk about the Leafs. It amazes me how loyal people still are to the team. And I'm no different. When I was away playing in the WHA, I still cheered for them to win. I remember getting excited in 1978 when they beat the Islanders and made it to the semifinals. I'm sure the fans who left the Leafs will come back if they can win again.

Right now the Leafs remind me of a big ocean liner in the middle of the water. They want to turn the ship around. The trouble is, you can't turn an ocean liner like a racing car. The process will be slow and often frustrating. You can never win with bad management. Just check out the Leafs' past if you need proof of this. But with Cliff Fletcher, Bill Watters, Darryl Sittler, and new coach Pat Burns in charge the ship's course will be righted. Having a great player like Darryl in the front office will rub off positively on everyone. It's good to see Darryl home where he belongs.

ON THE NHL TODAY

With my busy schedule I don't get as many chances as I would like to attend NHL games. From what I've seen there are some very noticeable differences from my day. The most obvious is the speed of the game. It's much faster than ever. The transition from defence to offence is the most dramatic. The other striking difference is the size of the players. They're much bigger and stronger. All the teams want large wingers to go into the corners and act as grinders. Teams dump the puck into the corners and the bangers have to go in and fish it out. They practise doing this. You don't see as many players carry the puck over the opposition's blue line anymore.

It looks as if almost every player can shoot the puck. There are so many more players with a heavy shot playing in the league compared to when I played. This is, in part, due to a change in the style of game played today. A

more offensive type of play is led by very mobile defencemen who are as intent on scoring and setting up goals as
they are on stopping them. Until Bobby Orr came along
most defencemen worried about their own end. Bobby
added a whole new dimension to the game.

I've also noticed more intensity out on the ice. This
could be because the shifts are usually no longer than 50
seconds. Players know they're out for a quick turn, so
they want to have some immediate impact. When I
played, you had to pace yourself for a longer shift, sometimes as much as two minutes. I would get a dirty look
from Normie Ullman if I came off too early. Today the
coach gets nervous if a player is out there for more than a
minute.

Hockey is meant to be a physical game. A great game
includes bodychecking. I'm talking about clean hits, not
the stick work you see today. The players have lost respect for one another. When that happens, you see an in-
crease in stick work, cross-checking from behind, and
running the goalie. Naturally brawling is the result. I
think we've seen enough fighting. It may be time to take
it out of the game. The NHL has to think about what
kind of image it wants to portray.

As I advanced up the hockey ladder, I had to be physical to survive. You took the man out, but you didn't try
to destroy him. We learned to use our shoulders, hips,
and strength to play the body. There were some great
hitters in my era. Guys like Bobby Baun, Bill Gadsby, Leo
Boivin, and Marcel Pronovost could deliver a bone-
crunching, legal body check. There are some good hitters
today. I like Luke Richardson of Edmonton and Scott Stevens of New Jersey, who can both deliver solid hits with
their shoulders.

I don't believe today's players are overprotected with

equipment. For instance, I think adding the visor to the helmet is a good move. It's especially important for kids. If I had a young son playing hockey, I wouldn't let him do so without a visor. Eyes are too important to lose playing a game. When I play hockey now, I wear a visor and believe it to be a positive innovation.

The negative side is that players are raising their sticks higher and higher and hitting one another in the face. This sort of stick work has to stop at the minor levels. Also the idiocy of cross-checking an opponent from behind and knocking him into the boards has to be eliminated. The NHL is trying to get this stupidity out of the game, but the league clearly has to start earlier when the players are being trained at a young age. I've been involved with kids playing "penalty-free" hockey, a program initiated by the Hockey Development Centre of Ontario and sponsored by Esso, which rewards teams who play the game without taking penalties. As I said before, hockey is meant to be played physically. When you get hit hard but clean, the opponent should be respected. Hockey has to eliminate the unnecessary retaliation. The penalty-free concept promotes the skill and sportsmanship of the game to young people and will hopefully be a step in the right direction.

The equipment used today is far superior to that of yesterday. It's lighter, more flexible, and affords better protection, all of which helps to prevent injury. I know a little about this since the helmet helped me to survive. I was one of the first players in the NHL to don one on a full-time basis. Actually it was an accident that caused me to first wear protective headgear.

When I was with Detroit, teammate Doug Barkley hit me with a slap shot in the head. At first the doctors thought I had sustained a fractured skull. It turned out to be a severe concussion, but to be on the safe side the doctors made me wear a helmet to finish up the season. During this time, I got used to wearing the headgear, although I found it hot and irritating. My wife encouraged me to make the helmet part of my equipment and I gave the matter some serious thought.

At the start of the following year the Red Wings wanted me to drop the helmet. They thought I'd lose my nerve if I kept it on. I realized this was ridiculous. By now I knew the helmet could save me from serious injury, but I told the Red Wings that if it affected my playing I'd take it off. They never asked me, though.

There was no reason not to wear the helmet. I can think of three instances where the headgear definitely saved me. One night I went into the corner with Pat Stapleton of Chicago. Patty was never a dirty hockey player, but somehow I found myself hitting the back of my head on the ice. I was knocked out even with my helmet on! Without the helmet I would have certainly fractured my skull.

Another time in Boston I was coming off the ice after a long shift when Gilles Marotte took a slap shot. The Bruins were killing a penalty, and he tried to slap it out of his own end. Because I was tired my head was down and I wasn't watching the play. The shot hit the top of my helmet, bounced off, and ended up about 40 rows into the crowd. The puck would have hit me square in the forehead, and I might have been in serious trouble if I wasn't wearing the helmet.

The other notable occasion the headgear saved me was in Moscow. During the first game over there, I was tripped and went backwards into the end boards, knocking myself out cold. The helmet saved me from sustaining no more than a slight concussion. I was even able to convince Harry Sinden to let me play the rest of the game. If I hadn't had the helmet on, I would have missed the rest of the series as well as my greatest thrill as a hockey player. Interestingly there were only two other players on the 1972 Team Canada who wore helmets — Red Berenson and Stan Mikita. All the Russian players, of course, wore protective headgear.

Increases in salaries paid to NHL players are a step in the right direction. Athletes are very gifted people who work hard to reach the professional level. They need to get compensated accordingly. If you're one of the best in the world at something, you should be paid that way. Players are the ones who put people in the stands and in front of their TVs. Why shouldn't they get their share of television contracts, gate receipts, and concessions? The Gretzkys, Lemieuxs, Yzermans, and Hulls are the reason the game thrives. They deserve to be in the higher echelons of the salary scale.

As long as players like the ones mentioned are the pacesetters, the game will be in good shape financially. There must be money in hockey. Look at how much two groups were willing to pay for expansion franchises. They wouldn't pay that kind of money if they didn't see themselves making a profit down the road. The players deserve their share, since it is they who will sell the game in new centres like Ottawa and Tampa Bay.

I find it good to see players giving their times to worthwhile causes. Because I'm involved, I see players at golf tournaments on behalf of charities and at benefit events for various organizations. At the recent Bobby Orr Skate-A-Thon held at Maple Leaf Gardens quite a few Leaf players were in attendance on a day off for them. Others take time to visit kids in hospital. With so much negative news about pro athletes out today it's nice to see that players still have time for the community.

If I were to advise a young man about playing in the NHL, I'd tell him to wait until he was physically and mentally mature to play at the top level and then would encourage him to go the university route, since I think it's important to complete your education. At the same time you need someone to give you an honest assessment of your skills and personality. Pro hockey isn't for everyone. For those with the right ingredients I wouldn't hesitate to tell them that playing in the NHL is a great experience. It can set you up for life. Expansion creates the need for more players. The competition will be tough, but the opportunities will be there.

ON EXPANSION IN THE NHL

I started my pro career in a minor league town that eventually became part of the NHL's first major expansion in 1967. Pittsburgh was a good hockey town in the early sixties when I played there. A new building was the main ingredient for a potential major league franchise. In 1991 Pittsburgh won the Stanley Cup for the first time, and in 1992 they repeated their success.

From a player's perspective expansion is always welcome. When the first expansion occurred in 1967, the fear of being sent down to the minors diminished considerably. Many new NHL jobs were created. These factors still hold true now that the NHL has expanded to 24 teams. With more jobs and more money available, kids will see a reason to stay involved with hockey. Considering the slow growth of our population, we'll need a larger number of youngsters who see hockey as a career they can aspire to.

Expansion is a double-edged sword. With each addition the quality of play in the league gets watered down a little more. This isn't good for the fans. The great rivalries of the past, like that of Toronto and Montreal, are gone. These teams rarely play each other anymore during the season, although other rivalries are developing, such as the one between the New York Rangers and the New Jersey Devils, or the fierce competition between the Los Angeles Kings and the Edmonton Oilers. Fans also like to identify with the players. With the vast numbers of players now in the NHL hidden behind equipment like helmets and visors, it's no wonder people don't know who they're watching. There is a definite downside to more expansion.

However, if a city can support an NHL team, I think they deserve one. There are obvious economic benefits to each town that can sustain an NHL franchise. In Canada expansion hockey is a little easier to sell because we love the game. In the United States the expansion teams will have to get competitive quickly. The U.S. markets will demand a winner. But the game will benefit if hockey can make it in new U.S. cities.

Marketing is also an important factor. The San Jose Sharks did a great job marketing their merchandise and logo. For an expansion team they were reasonably competitive in their first year of operation, and it will be interesting to see if the new teams will be able to match their success.

ON SOME HOCKEY PLAYERS I ADMIRE

Jean Beliveau could do it all as a hockey player, and I'll always remember him as a sportsman. Beliveau was a gentleman when the word meant something. He played and conducted himself in such a classy manner that it made him representative of what hockey should be all about. If there was someone I wanted to be like, it was Jean Beliveau. I can't think of a better role model.

Bobby Baun always played tough, but he was never a dirty hockey player. He stuck his nose in there every game. I played with and against Tim Horton, and he always had my utmost respect. He was a man of great strength and had a wonderful sense of humour. Ron Ellis was the consummate team player, who was more concerned about his own end than about his personal statistics. He worked hard at being a good two-way player and was a key ingredient in our win over the Russians in 1972. Larry Hillman was a player who got a great deal out of his abilities. A dedicated worker with a great work ethic, he never complained. His attitude made him a popular guy on every team he played with, and the Stanley Cup seemed to follow him around to Detroit, Toronto, and Montreal. Norm Ullman was a gifted hockey player. An intense competitor, he played the game like a sportsman and was one of the best forecheckers in the game. I was fortunate to play most of my career with this Hall of Famer.

Stan Mikita was a wonderful playmaker with great moves. He changed the way he played the game, but it never took away from his competitive nature. Bobby Orr was one of the smoothest players I've ever seen and my choice as the all-time best defenceman. Bobby was a tremendous passer, skater, and shooter; he did it all.

As for players today, I'd like to play one game of hockey with Wayne Gretzky's or Mario Lemieux's skills. Mario's moves are so incredible that his goals look like works of art. Both these players have raised the game to a new level. It doesn't matter in what era these two played; they would always dominate.

ON INTERNATIONAL HOCKEY

It's safe to say the 1972 series changed the way Canadians look at hockey. The Russians made us sit back and examine our game. With their five-man attack units the Soviets played a very controlled game. They carried the puck into the offensive zone, which allowed them to display their superior passing and playing skills. How many times did they finish a play by putting a puck into an almost empty net? We were hard-pressed to match their discipline and skill level. I think we also learned a great deal about conditioning. Our players now work at staying in shape year-round. Training camps are no longer used to shed extra pounds. Players arrive ready to go full out.

All the countries that compete in international hockey have become students of the Canadian game. They understand the need to become tougher and to play with more emotion just as we did in 1972. Being skilled isn't enough. You need heart, character, and desire to win at any level of competition. I think Canadians have always shown themselves to be leaders in playing with intense determination.

The country to watch in the future will be the United States. In the 1970s there were probably more Europeans playing pro hockey in North America than there were Americans, but that is starting to change. U.S.-born players are now stars in the NHL. Players like Pat LaFontaine, Jeremy Roenick, Brian Leetch, and Mike Richter are all premier players. In the 1991 Canada Cup the Americans made it to the finals for the first time, which could be a sign of things to come.

A short while ago I was talking to someone who had just watched a minor hockey tournament that included Canadian and American bantams. He told me the American kids were much more disciplined than the Canadian boys. They could control their tempers. Obviously their coaches spend time teaching the players to maintain their self-control and stay away from bad penalties. Perhaps the Americans are like this because they play more of other sports like football and basketball, which require a high level of discipline. Canadians make too many allowances for rough play. We have to learn to control our emotions on the ice.

If Canada is going to retain its status as a hockey power, we'll have to encourage young people to stay in the game. Too many youngsters are getting beat up on the ice. They don't want to put up with it, so they go into other sports. There's a boy of 15 living close to my house who plays at about 135 pounds. He has to go up against kids who might be 180 pounds and, of course, he gets nailed out there. Nobody lets up on him. I know they have to take him out of the play, but do they have to kill him? I find it hard to understand. The boy's parents are obviously concerned for their son.

Smaller boys are backing away from hockey. I think the game has been better for having little guys like Dave Keon, Henri Richard, Stan Mikita, and Denis Savard playing their brand of hockey. The smaller players bring a certain style and skill the game needs. I hope they don't get eliminated in the future. I'd hate to see the diminutive kids quit the game. With the right coaching playing hockey can be a great learning experience for young people.

I'm proud to say Canadians are still the top hockey players in the world. When you consider our population, it's amazing that Canada is the number one hockey nation. We have won four of the five Canada Cup tournaments with some great efforts in close games. I like to think back to the 1987 Canada Cup when we played a three-game final against the Soviets. Those were great hockey games. I was at the final game with Ron Ellis, and when Canada was down 3-0, I turned to Ronnie and said, "Somebody's going to have to do something to get us going and the referee has to give us some slack." Then Mark Messier hammered a Russian with an elbow at centre ice, and that got the Canadian team fired up enough to come back and win 6-5 on Mario Lemieux's brilliant goal, following Wayne Gretzky's pass. It was a typical Canadian victory!

In the future, if Canada wants to retain its international position in hockey, we'll have to use our best pros. For the Olympic Games and the World Championships we need our top players to have a realistic chance at winning. Let's face it, other countries have practically caught up to Canada when it comes to playing hockey. International hockey isn't an unknown product anymore. We know what we're up against. Somehow we have to find ways to let the best Canadians compete in these events.

ON THE SOVIET UNION

On the day they announced the end of the Soviet Union as we knew it, I was listening to the radio in my car when the telephone rang. A friend of mine, Gary Alles, called to see if I'd heard the news. We talked about it for a few minutes and then Gary said, "You know, Paul, it was you who started all this."

"What are you talking about?" I asked, a little puzzled.

"When you scored the goal, it was the beginning of the end for the Russians. They never recovered!"

We chuckled over that one for a few minutes.

Since 1972 I've been over to the former USSR on a number of occasions, including a period just before the attempted overthrow of Mikhail Gorbachev. In fact, just recently I returned from another trip to Russia. All of these trips have given me the opportunity to get to know the Russian people. In 1972 I don't think I had any use for Russians, but I changed my mind as I got to know them better.

The average Russian is a very gentle, humble person with a good heart. They have been misunderstood for a long time. All they wanted was some freedom and to have the ability to put food on the table. They want space to raise their children. Like anyone who lives in Canada, they want to give their kids what they didn't have. I've done a lot of travelling, and I can tell you the Russian people have as much character as any Canadian or American. We used to laugh at their propaganda, thinking we were so much better than they were. Their wants and desires are no different from ours. I have great respect for them as people.

They also have their share of sports fans. When you start talking sports, their eyes light up. This is the great thing about a game — it can bring people together from any part of the world. The Russians also like to eat, drink, and have a good time. During a recent visit, I was taken out for dinner. They had a big spread of food prepared for us and, of course, the vodka was flowing for them. We sang songs and had a very pleasurable evening. I found them to be very down-to-earth people.

At the moment there is a tremendous amount of freedom in the former Soviet republics. I've been over there to teach them about spiritual things, and I've had far more liberty than I do in this country. I can walk into their schools and give out Bibles without any problems. They think we have a great society because we have the freedom to practise religion and to believe in God. They want to learn about the Lord and they know what happens when there is no spiritual basis to act from. The Russian people are very open and inquisitive. They want to understand certain concepts they've never had a chance to examine before, and I always found them to be respectful of what we were sharing. There's probably more openness in the former Soviet Union than in Canada right now, where we have to worry about what every minority group might think before we can say something. Perhaps we've lost sight of some basic democratic principles.

I've also dealt with Russian athletes. The Moscow Dynamo hockey team invited us to speak to the players about Christianity. I shared my faith with them and we tried to help them understand the Bible. We were treated with great respect and their hospitality was tremendous.

The breakup of the Soviet Union is quite frightening in many ways. There is a great deal of turmoil, which I see continuing for some time. Their economic structure is getting worse and is now victimized by an ever-burgeoning black market and the proliferation of organized crime. I've heard that as little as ten percent of the food gets to where it's supposed to go. They have profiteers out there just as we do, and the road ahead for them isn't going to be easy.

ON THE 1972 SERIES
As people, Canadians learned a great deal about themselves from the 1972 series. When our pride is on the line, we never give up. It looked pretty bleak for us, but as long as we had a chance we kept on battling. The fat lady was warming up, but she never got a chance to sing. As the team fought back, Canadians rallied to our side. The support helped us reach down for a little more when we thought there was nothing left. I think we showed we aren't a nation of quitters.

While I write this the discussion of whether Canada

will survive as a country continues. It saddens me even to think of Canada disintegrating into various parts. I look at my grandson Josh and see how he views his heritage. He was born and lives in the U.S. He comes to Canada to spend time in the summer with his grandparents. "I'm an American," he says proudly. It's something that has been instilled in him. Americans like to boast about their nation. In Canada we don't seem to have this pride and love of country, and it irritates me to no end to see the disrespect Canadians show when our national anthem is played. We may fall apart if we don't foster a deeper devotion to Canada. The 1972 team drew together because we had the bigger cause in mind — win for Canada. There were no easterners, westerners, or Quebeckers on the team, only Canadian hockey players. Nobody had a separate agenda. If we did, Canada would have lost the series.

We have one of the most beautiful countries in the world. I don't understand why some people are trying to break it up, although I can see how certain historical wrongs have frustrated some. Canadians need to sit back and look at the big picture. Our unity is perhaps Canada's greatest asset. We proved it in 1972.

Over the years there has been talk of organizing another eight-game series between Canada and what was once the Soviet Union. With the breakup of the USSR I don't know if it would be possible, but I would love to see it. I think it would make for some incredible hockey. To see players like Mario Lemieux, Wayne Gretzky, Paul Coffey, Al MacInnis, Luc Robitaille, Eric Lindros, and Patrick Roy play in such a series would be great for the fans. The Unified Team showed it is still at the top of the class in international hockey by winning a gold medal at the 1992 Olympics, and when they play Canada's best, they should be allowed to use any NHL player born in the Commonwealth of Independent States.

I don't think a new series would tarnish the memory of 1972. Nothing could possibly match the emotion of the original. It would also be nice to see Canadians go over and win in Moscow as we did. No team of Canadian professionals has been able to win it all in the former USSR since 1972.

Now that the 20th anniversary of the series has arrived, I'm looking forward to all the renewed interest in those incredible days. A company has put out a series of 100 cards based on the 1972 series and, as I flip through them, the memories come flooding back. It was a great time to be a Canadian, and I'll always remember the event as a very positive force in my life.

ON MY FAMILY AND LIFE TODAY

On January 28, 1993, I'll celebrate my 50th birthday, while in 1992 Eleanor and I will commemorate our 30th wedding anniversary. We're going to have a family get-together to mark both occasions. We have much to be thankful for. The family has grown over the years, but we're as close as ever.

Two of our daughters are married and live in the United States. Heather is now 29 and resides in New Mexico with her husband, Alex, a pilot in the U.S. Air Force. They have two boys, Brandon and Zachary. Jennifer, 27, is married to Mike, and they live in Birmingham, Alabama, with their son Josh. Mike is contemplating a job offer that might take them to Dallas. We'd be really happy if both families would move to the northeastern United States; it would be nice to have the family closer geographically. However, Jill, 22, lives with us in our

Mississauga home and attends Ryerson College in Toronto, where she studies interior design.

One day I asked Jill what was the most positive thing we had done for her as parents. She quickly said the respect we showed her was extremely important. This admission surprised me somewhat, since it wasn't what I had expected. "You gave us freedom to make our choices, and we knew you were always there for us and we knew we were loved. We respected you because you showed respect for us," Jill told me. As a parent, I don't think I could ask for anything more.

Christianity has had a major impact on the lives of everyone in my family. Many of our friends, too, have become Christians through our experience, although certainly not all of them. I enjoy helping people understand Christianity because I believe it can make a difference in the life they lead. When I first started out with my ministry, it was with some trepidation. As I saw the impact of my work on people, I began to feel very good about what I was doing with my life. Now I can see positive changes in men as husbands and fathers, and I think I'm making a contribution to society.

Eleanor spends a fair amount of time working with me at the ministry. She helps out in the office and gets me organized. It's good to share this second career with her. I've only had two real jobs in my life, and Eleanor has enjoyed both. She has always been helpful to me. I couldn't have made a better choice for a wife. I can honestly say Eleanor is the best woman in the world for me. We pray together in the morning and thank the Lord for all He has given us, including a marriage that has now lasted 30 years. We have also been able to make many good friends over the years, which has enriched our lives.

If it all ended tomorrow, we could still say it was a wonderful life.

I have no intention of stopping or slowing down. I'm going to enjoy life to the fullest. After all, I still have the Goal stories to hear. One morning not so long ago I had my car radio tuned to CFRB radio in Toronto. Broadcasters Pat Marsden and Jim Hunt were talking about their greatest moment in sports. They both picked the 1972 series and the Goal as the highlight of their careers. It happened 20 years ago, but people haven't forgotten.

The athletic highlight of my career was participating in the 1972 series and scoring the winning goal. The fame helped me to realize my early ambitions in life. I started out in search of the good life and money. Fortunately the aftermath of the series helped me to reexamine my life. It gave me the impetus to take a new direction, causing my goals and aspirations to change. I started to ask the important questions and I began to care about what I would leave behind.

Becoming a Christian hasn't made me perfect by any means. I have faults like anybody else, but I do have a great feeling of contentment. I enjoy who I am and I can honestly tell you I wouldn't change places with anyone.

11

Statistics and Summaries

PAUL GARNET HENDERSON
Born January 28, 1943, Kincardine, Ontario
5'11", 180 lbs. Left Wing, Shoots Right
Junior Club: Hamilton Red Wings

YEAR	TEAM	LEAGUE	GP	G	A	PTS	PIM
1962-63	Detroit	NHL	2	0	0	0	9
1963-64	Detroit	NHL	32	3	3	6	6
1964-65	Detroit	NHL	70	8	13	21	30
1965-66	Detroit	NHL	69	22	24	46	34
1966-67	Detroit	NHL	46	21	19	40	12
1967-68	Detroit	NHL	50	13	20	33	35
1967-68	Toronto	NHL	13	5	6	11	8
1968-69	Toronto	NHL	74	27	32	59	16
1969-70	Toronto	NHL	67	20	22	42	18
1970-71	Toronto	NHL	72	30	30	60	34
1971-72	Toronto	NHL	73	38	20	58	32
1972-73	Toronto	NHL	40	18	16	34	18
1973-74	Toronto	NHL	69	24	31	55	40
1974-75	Toronto	WHA	58	30	33	63	18
1975-76	Toronto	WHA	65	26	29	55	22
1976-77	Birmingham	WHA	81	23	25	48	30
1977-78	Birmingham	WHA	80	37	29	66	22
1978-79	Birmingham	WHA	76	24	27	51	20
1979-80	Atlanta	NHL	30	7	6	13	6
CAREER		NHL:	707	236	242	478	296
TOTALS		WHA:	360	140	143	283	112

PLAYOFFS

YEAR	TEAM	LEAGUE	GP	G	A	PTS	PIM
1963-64	Detroit	NHL	14	2	3	5	6
1964-65	Detroit	NHL	7	0	2	2	0
1965-66	Detroit	NHL	12	3	3	6	10
1968-69	Toronto	NHL	4	0	1	1	0
1970-71	Toronto	NHL	6	5	1	6	4
1971-72	Toronto	NHL	5	1	2	3	6
1973-74	Toronto	NHL	4	0	2	2	2
1977-78	Birmingham	WHA	5	1	1	2	0
1979-80	Atlanta	NHL	4	0	0	0	0
CAREER		NHL:	56	11	14	25	28
TOTALS		WHA:	5	1	1	2	0

1972 CANADA — SOVIET SERIES

CANADA

COACHES

Harry Sinden
John Ferguson

GOALTENDERS

1. Ed Johnston, Boston
29. Ken Dryden, Montreal
35. Tony Esposito, Chicago

DEFENCEMEN

2. Gary Bergman, Detroit
3. Pat Stapleton, Chicago
4. Bobby Orr, Boston
5. Brad Park, New York
16. Rod Seiling, New York
17. Bill White, Chicago
23. Serge Savard, Montreal
25. Guy Lapointe, Montreal
26. Don Awrey, Boston
37. Jocelyn Guevremont, Vancouver
38. Brian Glennie, Toronto

FORWARDS

6. Ron Ellis, Toronto
7. Phil Esposito, Boston, A
8. Rodrigue Gilbert, New York
9. Bill Goldsworthy, Minnesota
10. Dennis Hull, Chicago
11. Vic Hadfield, New York
12. Yvan Cournoyer, Montreal
14. Wayne Cashman, Boston
15. Red Berenson, Detroit
18. Jean Ratelle, New York, A
19. Paul Henderson, Toronto
20. Peter Mahovlich, Montreal
21. Stan Mikita, Chicago, A
22. Jean-Paul Parise, Minnesota
24. Mickey Redmond, Detroit
27. Frank Mahovlich, Montreal, A
28. Bobby Clarke, Philadelphia
32. Dale Tallon, Vancouver
33. Gilbert Perreault, Buffalo
34. Marcel Dionne, Detroit
36. Richard Martin, Buffalo
A = Team Captains

SOVIET UNION

COACHES

Vsevolod Bobrov
Boris Kulagin

GOALTENDERS

20. Vladislav Tretiak
27. Alexander Sidelnikov

DEFENCEMEN

2. Alexander Gusev
3. Vladimir Lutchenko
4. Victor Kuzkin
5. Alexander Ragulin
6. Valeri Vasiliev
7. Gennady Tsygankov
14. Yuri Shatalov
25. Yuri Liapkin
26. Yevgeny Paladiev

FORWARDS

8. Vyacheslav Starshinov
9. Yuri Blinov
10. Alexander Maltsev
11. Yevgeny Zimin
12. Yevgeny Mishakov
13. Boris Mikhailov
15. Alexander Yakushev
16. Vladimir Petrov
17. Valeri Kharlamov
18. Vladimir Vikulov
19. Vladimir Shadrin
21. Vyacheslav Solodukhin
22. Vyacheslav Anisin
23. Yuri Lebedev
24. Alexander Bodunov
29. Alexander Martynyuk
30. Alexander Volchkov

GAME SUMMARIES

GAME 1
SEPTEMBER 2 AT MONTREAL —
SOVIET UNION 7, TEAM CANADA 3

FIRST PERIOD

1. TEAM CANADA	P. Esposito (F. Mahovlich, Bergman)	0:30
2. TEAM CANADA	Henderson (Clarke)	6:32
3. SOVIET UNION	Zimin (Yakushev, Shadrin)	11:40
4. SOVIET UNION	Petrov (Mikhailov)	(SHG) 17:28

PENALTIES: Henderson (C) (tripping) 1:03; Yakushev (S) (tripping) 7:04, Mikhailov (S) (tripping) 15:11; Ragulin (S) (tripping) 17:19

SECOND PERIOD

5. SOVIET UNION	Kharlamov (Maltsev)	2:40
6. SOVIET UNION	Kharlamov (Maltsev)	(GWG) 10:18

PENALTIES: Clarke (C) (slashing) 5:16, Lapointe (C) (slashing) 12:53

THIRD PERIOD

7. TEAM CANADA	Clarke (Ellis, Henderson)	8:22
8. SOVIET UNION	Mikhailov (Blinov)	13:32
9. SOVIET UNION	Zimin (unassisted)	14:29
10. SOVIET UNION	Yakushev (Shadrin)	18:37

PENALTIES: Kharlamov (S) (high-sticking) 14:45; Lapointe (C) (cross-checking) 19:41

Shots on goal by:	SOVIET UNION	10	10	10	30
	TEAM CANADA	10	10	12	32

Goaltenders:	SOVIET UNION	Tretiak, 60 minutes, 3 goals against
	TEAM CANADA	Dryden, 60 minutes, 7 goals against

Attendance:	18,818

GAME 2
SEPTEMBER 4 AT TORONTO —
TEAM CANADA 4, SOVIET UNION 1

FIRST PERIOD

No scoring

PENALTIES: Park (C) (cross-checking) 10:08; Henderson (C) (tripping) 15:09

SECOND PERIOD

1. TEAM CANADA	P. Esposito (Park, Cashman)	7:14

PENALTIES: Gusev (S) (tripping) 2:07; Soviet Union bench minor 4:13; Bergman (C) (tripping) 15:16; Tsygankov (S) (slashing) 19:54; Kharlamov (S) (misconduct) 19:54

THIRD PERIOD

2. TEAM CANADA	Cournoyer (Park)	(PPG) (GWG) 1:19
3. SOVIET UNION	Yakushev (Lapkin, Zimin)	(PPG) 5:53
4. TEAM CANADA	P. Mahovlich (P. Esposito)	(SHG) 6:47
5. TEAM CANADA	F. Mahovlich (Mikita, Cournoyer)	8:59

PENALTIES: Clarke (C) (slashing) 5:13; Stapleton (C) (hooking) 6:14

Shots on goal by:	SOVIET UNION	7	5	9	21
	TEAM CANADA	10	16	10	36

Goaltenders:	SOVIET UNION	Tretiak, 60 minutes, 4 goals against
	TEAM CANADA	T. Esposito, 60 minutes, 1 goal against

Attendance:	16,485

GAME 3
SEPTEMBER 6 AT WINNIPEG —
SOVIET UNION 4, TEAM CANADA 4

FIRST PERIOD

1. TEAM CANADA	Parise (White, P. Esposito)		1:54
2. SOVIET UNION	Petrov (unassisted)	(SHG)	3:16
3. TEAM CANADA	Ratelle (Cournoyer, Bergman)		18:25

PENALTIES: Vasiliev (S) (elbowing) 3:02; Cashman (C) (slashing) 8:01; Parise (C) (interference) 15:47

SECOND PERIOD

4. TEAM CANADA	P. Esposito (Cashman, Parise)		4:19
5. SOVIET UNION	Kharlamov (Tsygankov)	(SHG)	12:56
6. TEAM CANADA	Henderson (Clarke, Ellis)		13:47
7. SOVIET UNION	Lebedev (Vasiliev, Anisin)		14:59
8. SOVIET UNION	Bodunov (Anisin)		18:28

PENALTIES: Petrov (S) (interference) 4:46; Lebedev (S) (tripping) 11:00

THIRD PERIOD

No scoring

PENALTIES: White (C) (slashing), Mishakov (S) (slashing) 1:33; Cashman (C) (slashing, misconduct) 10:44

Shots on goal by:	SOVIET UNION	9	8	8	25
	TEAM CANADA	15	17	6	38

Goaltenders:	SOVIET UNION	Tretiak, 60 minutes, 4 goals against
	TEAM CANADA	T. Esposito, 60 minutes, 4 goals against

Attendance: 9,800

GAME 4
SEPTEMBER 8 AT VANCOUVER —
SOVIET UNION 5, TEAM CANADA 3

FIRST PERIOD

1. SOVIET UNION	Mikhailov (Lutchenko, Petrov)	(PPG)	2:01
2. SOVIET UNION	Mikhailov (Lutchenko, Petrov)	(PPG)	7:29

PENALTIES: Goldsworthy (C) (cross-checking) 1:24; Goldsworthy (C) (elbowing) 5:58; P. Esposito (C) (tripping) 19:29

SECOND PERIOD

3. TEAM CANADA	Perreault (unassisted)		5:37
4. SOVIET UNION	Blinov (Petrov, Mikhailov)		6:34
5. SOVIET UNION	Vikulov (Kharlamov, Maltsev)	(GWG)	13:52

PENALTY: Kuzkin (S) (tripping) 8:39

THIRD PERIOD

6. TEAM CANADA	Goldsworthy (P. Esposito, Bergman)		6:54
7. SOVIET UNION	Shadrin (Yakushev, Vasiliev)		11:05
8. TEAM CANADA	Hull (P. Esposito, Goldsworthy)	19:38	

PENALTY: Petrov (S) (holding) 2:01

Shots on goal by:	SOVIET UNION	11	14	6	31
	TEAM CANADA	10	8	23	41

Goaltenders:	SOVIET UNION	Tretiak, 60 minutes, 3 goals against
	TEAM CANADA	Dryden, 60 minutes, 5 goals against

Attendance:	15,570

GAME 5
SEPTEMBER 22 AT MOSCOW —
SOVIET UNION 5, TEAM CANADA 4

FIRST PERIOD

1. TEAM CANADA	Parise (Perreault, Gilbert)	15:30

PENALTIES: Ellis (C) (tripping) 3:49; Kharlamov (S) (slashing) 12:25

SECOND PERIOD

2. TEAM CANADA	Clarke (Henderson)	2:36
3. TEAM CANADA	Henderson (Lapointe, Clarke)	11:58

PENALTIES: Ellis (C) (slashing) 5:38, Kharlamov (S) (holding) 5:38; Bergman (C) (roughing) 8:13; White (C) (slashing), Blinov (S) (slashing) 20:00

THIRD PERIOD

4. SOVIET UNION	Blinov, (Petrov, Kuzkin)	3:34
5. TEAM CANADA	Henderson (Clarke)	4:56
6. SOVIET UNION	Anisin (Liapkin, Yakushev)	9:05
7. SOVIET UNION	Shadrin (Anisin)	9:13
8. SOVIET UNION	Gusev (Ragulin, Kharlamov)	11:41
9. SOVIET UNION	Vikulov (Kharlamov)	(GWG) 14:46

PENALTIES: Clarke (C) (holding) 10:25; Tsygankov (S) (high-sticking) 10:25; Yakushev (S) (hooking) 15:48

Shots on goal by:	SOVIET UNION	9	13	11	33
	TEAM CANADA	12	13	12	37

Goaltenders:	SOVIET UNION	Tretiak, 60 minutes, 4 goals against
	TEAM CANADA	T. Esposito, 60 minutes, 5 goals against

Attendance:	15,000

GAME 6
SEPTEMBER 24 AT MOSCOW —
TEAM CANADA 3, SOVIET UNION 2

FIRST PERIOD

No scoring

PENALTIES: Bergman (C) (tripping) 10:21; P. Esposito (C) (double minor, charging) 13:11

SECOND PERIOD

1. SOVIET UNION	Liapkin (Yakushev, Shadrin)	1:12
2. TEAM CANADA	Hull (Gilbert)	5:13
3. TEAM CANADA	Cournoyer (Berenson)	6:21
4. TEAM CANADA	Henderson (unassisted)	(GWG) 6:36
5. SOVIET UNION	Yakushev (Shadrin, Liapkin)	(PPG) 17:11

PENALTIES: Ragulin (S) (interference) 2:09; Lapointe (C) (roughing), Vasiliev (S) (roughing) 8:29; Clarke (C) (slashing, misconduct) 10:12; D. Hull (C) (slashing) 17:02; P. Esposito (C) (high-sticking major) 17:46; Team Canada bench minor 17:46

THIRD PERIOD

No scoring

PENALTY: Ellis (C) (holding) 17:39

Shots on goal by:	SOVIET UNION	6	13	12	31
	TEAM CANADA	9	7	9	25

Goaltenders:	SOVIET UNION	Tretiak, 60 minutes, 3 goals against
	TEAM CANADA	Dryden, 60 minutes, 2 goals against

Attendance:	15,000

GAME 7
SEPTEMBER 26 AT MOSCOW —
TEAM CANADA 4, SOVIET UNION 3

FIRST PERIOD

1. TEAM CANADA	P. Esposito (Ellis, Henderson)	4:09
2. SOVIET UNION	Yakushev (Shadrin, Liapkin)	10:17
3. SOVIET UNION	Petrov (Vikulov, Tsygankov)	(PPG) 16:27
4. TEAM CANADA	P. Esposito (Savard, Parise)	(SHG) 17:34

PENALTIES: Mikhailov (S) (tripping) 2:00; P. Mahovlich (C) (roughing), Mishakov (S) (holding) 5:16; Mishakov (S) (holding) 11:09; P. Esposito (C) (cross-checking) 12:39; White (C) (interference) 15:45

SECOND PERIOD

No scoring

PENALTIES: Gilbert (C) (hooking) 0:59; Parise (C) (slashing) 6:04; Anisin (S) (hooking) 6:11; P. Esposito (C) (roughing), Kuzkin (S) (roughing) 12:44; Parise (C) (roughing), Kuzkin (S) (roughing) 15:14; Stapleton (C) (holding) 15:24

THIRD PERIOD

5. TEAM CANADA	Gilbert (Ratelle, Hull)	2:13
6. SOVIET UNION	Yakushev (Maltsev, Lutchenko)	(PPG) 5:15
7. TEAM CANADA	Henderson (Savard)	(GWG) 17:54

PENALTIES: Bergman (C) (holding) 3:26; Gilbert (C) (charging) 7:25; Bergman (C) (roughing major), Mikhailov (S) (roughing major) 16:26

Shots on goal by:	SOVIET UNION		6	13	12	31
	TEAM CANADA		9	7	9	25

Goaltenders:	SOVIET UNION	Tretiak, 60 minutes, 4 goals against
	TEAM CANADA	T. Esposito, 60 minutes, 3 goals against

Attendance:	15,000

GAME 8
SEPTEMBER 28 AT MOSCOW —
TEAM CANADA 6, SOVIET UNION 5

FIRST PERIOD

1. SOVIET UNION	Yakushev (Maltsev, Liapkin)	(PPG) 3:34
2. TEAM CANADA	P. Esposito (Park)	(PPG) 6:45
3. SOVIET UNION	Lutchenko (Kharlamov)	(PPG)13:10
4. TEAM CANADA	Park (Ratelle, Hull)	16:59

PENALTIES: White (C) (holding) 2:25; P. Mahovlich (C) (holding) 3:01; Petrov (S) (hooking) 3:44; Parise (C) (interference, misconduct, game misconduct) 4:10; Tsygankov (S) (interference) 6:28; Ellis (C) (interference) 9:27; Petrov (S) (interference) 9:46; Cournoyer (C) (interference) 12:51

SECOND PERIOD

5. SOVIET UNION	Shadrin (unassisted)	0:21
6. TEAM CANADA	White (Gilbert, Ratelle)	10:32
7. SOVIET UNION	Yakushev (unassisted)	11:43
8. SOVIET UNION	Vasiliev (unassisted)	(PPG) 16:44

PENALTIES: Stapleton (C) (cross-checking) 15:58; Kuzkin (S) (elbowing) 18:06

THIRD PERIOD

9. TEAM CANADA	P. Esposito (P. Mahovlich)	2:27
10. TEAM CANADA	Cournoyer (P. Esposito, Park)	12:56
11. TEAM CANADA	Henderson (P. Esposito)	(GWG) 19:26

PENALTIES: Gilbert (C) (fighting major); Mishakov (S) (fighting major) 3:41; Vasiliev (S) (tripping) 4:27; Hull (C) (high-sticking), Petrov (S) (elbowing) 15:24

Shots on goal by:	SOVIET UNION		12	10	5	27
	TEAM CANADA		14	8	14	36

Goaltenders:	SOVIET UNION	Tretiak, 60 minutes, 6 goals against
	TEAM CANADA	Dryden, 60 minutes, 5 goals against

Attendance:	15,000

INDIVIDUAL STATISTICS

CANADA

PLAYER	GP	G	A	PTS	PIM
P. Esposito	8	7	6	13	15
Henderson	8	7	3	10	4
Clarke	8	2	4	6	18
Cournoyer	8	3	2	5	2
Park	8	1	4	5	2
Hull	4	2	2	4	4
Parise	6	2	2	4	28
Gilbert	6	1	3	4	9
Ratelle	6	1	3	4	0
Bergman	8	0	3	3	13
Ellis	8	0	3	3	8
Perreault	2	1	1	2	0
Goldsworthy	3	1	1	2	4
F. Mahovlich	6	1	1	2	0
P. Mahovlich	7	1	1	2	4
White	7	1	1	2	8
Cashman	2	0	2	2	14
Savard	5	0	2	2	0
Mikita	2	0	1	1	0
Berenson	2	0	1	1	0
Lapointe	7	0	1	1	6
Redmond	1	0	0	0	0
Awrey	2	0	0	0	0
Hadfield	2	0	0	0	0
Seiling	3	0	0	0	0
Stapleton	7	0	0	0	6
TOTALS	8	31	46	77	147

SOVIET UNION

PLAYER	GP	G	A	PTS	PIM
Yakushev	8	7	4	11	4
Shadrin	8	3	5	8	0
Kharlamov	7	3	4	7	16
Petrov	8	3	4	7	10
Liapkin	6	1	5	6	0
Mikhailov	8	3	2	5	9
Maltsev	8	0	5	5	0
Anisin	7	1	3	4	2
Lutchenko	8	1	3	4	0
Zimin	2	2	1	3	0
Blinov	5	2	1	3	2
Vikulov	6	2	1	3	0
Vasiliev	6	1	2	3	6
Tsygankov	8	0	2	2	6
Lebedev	3	1	0	1	2
Bodunov	3	1	0	1	0
Gusev	6	1	0	1	2
Ragulin	6	0	1	1	4
Kuzkin	7	0	1	1	8
Martynyuk	1	0	0	0	0
Solodukhin	1	0	0	0	0
Starshinov	1	0	0	0	0
Shatalov	2	0	0	0	0
Volchkov	3	0	0	0	0
Paladiev	3	0	0	0	0
Mishakov	6	0	0	0	11
TOTALS	8	32	44	76	84

TEAM STATISTICS

Goals by:	1st period	2nd period	3rd period	Total
Soviet Union	9	12	11	32
Team Canada	9	10	12	31

Shots on goal by:				
Soviet Union	76	81	70	227
Team Canada	87	87	93	267

Shots at goal by:				
Soviet Union	188	170	159	517
Team Canada	163	162	156	481

Total advantages:	Soviet Union	38	Team Canada	23
Power play goals:	Soviet Union	9	Team Canada	2
Shorthand goals:	Soviet Union	3	Team Canada	1
Penalty minutes:	Soviet Union	84	Team Canada	147

Goaltending Statistics

Player	Games	GA	Ave.
Esposito, Team Canada	4	13	3.25
Dryden, Team Canada	4	19	4.75
Tretiak, Soviet Union	8	31	3.87

1974 CANADA — SOVIET SERIES

CANADA

GOALTENDERS

1. Don McLeod
30. Gerry Cheevers

DEFENCEMEN

2. Rick Ley
3. J. C. Tremblay
6. Brad Selwood
10. Marty Howe
12. Pat Stapleton
17. Rick Smith
19. Paul Shmyr
24. Al Hamilton

FORWARDS

4. Mike Walton
5. Rejean Houle
7. Andre Lacroix
8. Tom Webster
9. Gordie Howe
11. Mark Howe
14. Ralph Backstrom
15. Jim Harrison
16. Bobby Hull
19. Paul Henderson
20. Bruce MacGregor
21. Serge Bernier
22. Marc Tardif
23. Johnny McKenzie
27. Frank Mahovlich

SOVIET UNION

GOALTENDERS

1. Alexander Sidelnikov
20. Vladislav Tretiak

DEFENCEMEN

2. Alexander Gusev
3. Vladimir Lutchenko
4. Jurl Shatalov
5. Juri Liapkin
6. Valeri Vasiliev
7. Gennady Tsygankov
12. Victor Kuznetsov
26. Alexander Fillppov
27. Alexander Sapelkin

FORWARDS

8. Sergei Kapustin
9. Alexander Volchkov
10. Alexander Maltsev
11. Yuri Lebedev
13. Boris Mikhailov
14. Vladimir Popov
15. Alexander Yakushev
16. Vladimir Petrov
17. Valery Kharlamov
19. Vladimir Shadrin
21. Vladimir Vikulov
22. Vyacheslav Anisin
24. Alexander Bodunov
29. Sergei Kotov
30. Konstantin Klimov
31. Victor Shalimov

GAME SUMMARIES

GAME 1
SEPTEMBER 17 AT QUEBEC CITY —
TEAM CANADA 3, SOVIET UNION 3

FIRST PERIOD

1. CANADA	McKenzie (Lacroix, Hull)	12:13

PENALTIES: None

SECOND PERIOD

2. RUSSIA	Lutchenko (Tsygankov, Kapustin)	7:46
3. CANADA	Hull (Walton, Howe)	12:07
4. RUSSIA	Kharlamov (Vasiliev)	14:04
5. RUSSIA	Petrov (Gusev, Kharlamov)	17:10

PENALTIES: Houle (tripping) 0:24; McKenzie (cross-checking), Liapkin (cross-check-ing) 4:24; Vasiliev (tripping) 11:07; Selwood (tripping) 12:40; Shmyr (tripping) 14:38 (cross-checking) 17:02.

THIRD PERIOD

6. CANADA	Hull (Lacroix, McKenzie)	14:18

PENALTIES: Kapuskin (holding) 6:04; Bodunov (hooking) 15:16

Shots on Goal:	Russia	8	11	9	28
	Canada	9	10	15	34

GAME 2
SEPTEMBER 19 AT TORONTO —
TEAM CANADA 4, SOVIET UNION 1

FIRST PERIOD

1. CANADA	Backstrom (Mark Howe, G. Howe)	4:31
2. CANADA	Lacroix (McKenzie, Tremblay)	10:49

PENALTIES: Smith (elbowing) 1:44; Kapustin (interference) 10:19; Kapustin (tripping) 12:50; Mahovlich (tripping) 16:08

SECOND PERIOD

3. CANADA	Hull (Lacroix, McKenzie)	2:50
4. RUSSIA	Yakushev (Shadrin, Lebedev)	13:09

PENALTIES: Mahovlich (slashing) 9:44; Lacroix (high-sticking) 15:39

THIRD PERIOD

5. CANADA	Tremblay (Lacroix, Hull)	17:03

PENALTIES: Smith (holding) 13:23; Maltsev (high-sticking) 16:04; Tremblay (high-sticking) 19:00

Shots on Goal					
	SOVIET UNION	13	8	9	30
	CANADA	10	16	7	33

GAME 3
SEPTEMBER 21 AT WINNIPEG —
SOVIET UNION 8, TEAM CANADA 5

FIRST PERIOD

1. CANADA	MacGregor (Henderson)	14:58
2. SOVIET UNION	Yakushev (Shadrin)	17:25

PENALTIES: Lacroix (slashing) 5:02; Smith (cross-checking) 13:25; Walton (tripping) 19:16

SECOND PERIOD

3. SOVIET UNION	Mikhailov (Petrov)	1:23
4. CANADA	Webster (Bernier, Tardif)	12:40
5. SOVIET UNION	Vasiliev (Mikhailov, Petrov)	15:14
6. SOVIET UNION	Maltsev (Anisin)	15:31

PENALTIES: Hamilton (cross-checking) 3:26; McKenzie, (roughing) 5:49; Kuznetsov (roughing) 5:49; Shadrin (slashing) 8:16; McKenzie, (roughing) 13:24; Lebedev (roughing) 13:24

THIRD PERIOD

7. SOVIET UNION	Yakushev (Shadrin)	2:35
8. SOVIET UNION	Bodunov	8:44
9. SOVIET UNION	Yakushev	11:27
10. CANADA	Henderson (Harrison)	14:31
11. CANADA	Henderson (Harrison, MacGregor)	15:04
12. CANADA	Bernier (Webster, Hamilton)	16:01
13. SOVIET UNION	Lebedev (Lutchenko)	18:05

PENALTIES: Kuznetsov (holding) 12:20; Lutchenko (tripping) 18:56

Shots on Goal					
	SOVIET UNION	11	16	12	39
	TEAM CANADA	8	14	12	34

GAME 4
SETPEMBER 23 AT VANCOUVER —
TEAM CANADA 5, SOVIET UNION 5

FIRST PERIOD

1. RUSSIA	Vasiliev (Kharlamov)	3:34
2. CANADA	G. Howe (Stapleton, Backstrom)	4:20
3. RUSSIA	Mikhailov (Petrov)	5:59
4. CANADA	Hull (Mahovlich)	12:45
5. CANADA	Hull (Stapleton)	15:11
6. CANADA	Mahovlich (Bernier, Houle)	17:10
7. CANADA	Hull (Lacroix)	17:45

PENALTY: Gusev (slashing) 11:38

SECOND PERIOD

8. RUSSIA	Yakushev (Lebedev)	11:04

PENALTIES: Shmyr (roughing) 4:08; Petrov (interference) 13:35; Smith (interference) 13:35; Ley (roughing) 17:07

THIRD PERIOD

9. RUSSIA	Maltsev	16:08
10. RUSSIA	Gusev (Mikhailov, Petrov)	16:59

PENALTIES: Shadrin (slashing) 6:45; McKenzie (elbowing) 7:30; McKenzie (hooking) 10:26; Tsygankov (tripping) 17:51

Shots on Goal	RUSSIA	12	10	6	28
	CANADA	11	8	9	28

GAME 5
OCTOBER 1 AT MOSCOW —
SOVIET UNION 3, TEAM CANADA 2

FIRST PERIOD

1. RUSSIA	Maltsev (Vikulov, Anisin)	4:34

PENALTIES: Mahovlich (holding) 2:32; Petrov (roughing) 6:59; Ley (roughing) 18:52; Bernier (roughing) 15:07

SECOND PERIOD

2. CANADA	G. Howe (Backstrom, Marty Howe)	00:15
3. RUSSIA	Maltsev (Shadrin, Vikulov)	15:04

PENALTIES: Webster (slashing) 4:14; Lebedev (high-sticking) 7:02; McKenzie (hooking) 13:52; Kharlamov (roughing) 18:52; Bernier (roughing) 18:52

THIRD PERIOD

4. RUSSIA	Gusev	11:48
5. CANADA	Mark Howe (Shmyr)	18:10

PENALTIES: Lacroix (slashing) 2:46; Backstrom (10-minute misconduct) 4:37; Shadrin (elbowing) 5:38; Bodunov (hooking) 16:21

Shots on Goal					
	Canada	8	4	4	16
	Russia	9	10	8	27

GAME 6
OCTOBER 3 AT MOSCOW —
SOVIET UNION 5, TEAM CANADA 2

FIRST PERIOD

1. RUSSIA	Mikhailov (Kharlamov)	0:34
2. RUSSIA	Vasiliev (Kharlamov)	2:43
3. CANADA	Houle (Shmyr)	15:56

PENALTIES: Mark Howe (cross-checking) 0:53; Smith (cross-checking) 16:38; Tardif (10-minute misconduct) 16:38

SECOND PERIOD

4. CANADA	G. Howe (Mark Howe)	6:15
5. RUSSIA	Anisin (Vikulov)	8:22
6. RUSSIA	Shatalov (Tsygankov)	13:57

PENALTIES: Mark Howe (cross-checking) 12:22; MacGregor (fighting) 12:44; Vasiliev (fighting) 12:44

THIRD PERIOD

7. RUSSIA	Kharlamov (Vikulov)	13:00

PENALTIES: Smith (slashing) 10:54; Kharlamov (slashing) 10:54; Lebedev (slashing) 15:04; Marty Howe (10-minute misconduct) 15:04; Ley (game misconduct) 20:00

Shots on Goal	Canada	13	9	6	28
	Russia	14	8	7	29

GAME 7
OCTOBER 5 AT MOSCOW —
CANADA 4, SOVIET UNION 4

FIRST PERIOD

1. RUSSIA	Anisin (Lutchenko)	3:34
2. RUSSIA	Tiurin (Lebedev, Yakushev)	6:47
3. CANADA	Webster (Lacroix)	17:42

PENALTIES: None

SECOND PERIOD

4. CANADA	Backstrom (G. Howe, Mark Howe)	2:55
5. CANADA	Mark Howe (Tremblay, Backstrom)	6:38
6. RUSSIA	Gusev (Petrov, Kharlamov)	7:20
7. RUSSIA	Mikhailov (Petrov, Kharlamov)	7:59

PENALTIES: Lutchenko (elbowing) 6:11; Stapleton (hooking) 7:06; Maltsev (interference) 9:18

THIRD PERIOD

8. CANADA	Backstrom (Tremblay)	6:38

PENALTIES: None

Shots on Goal	Canada	10	13	7	30
	Russia	11	7	3	21

GAME 8
OCTOBER 6 AT MOSCOW —
SOVIET UNION 3, TEAM CANADA 2

FIRST PERIOD

1. CANADA	Hull (Backstrom, Tremblay)	13:47

PENALTIES: Webster (roughing) 7:57; Yakushev (tripping) 13:08; Turin (holding) 15:26; Hamilton (elbowing) 18:21

SECOND PERIOD

2. RUSSIA	Yakushev (Shadrin)	6:27

PENALTIES: Popov (interference) 2:18; Ley (roughing) 2:18; Harrison (cross-checking) 6:12; Harrison (charging) 10:34; Harrison (slashing major) 18:10; Marty Howe (cross-checking) 19:03

THIRD PERIOD

3. RUSSIA	Shalimov	0:53
4. RUSSIA	Shalimov (Yakushev)	6:59
5. CANADA	Backstrom (G. Howe, Ley)	12:42

PENALTIES: Shadrin (high-sticking major), Stapleton (misconduct) 2:15; G. Howe (hooking) 7:50; Turin (tripping) 19:20; Canada (bench, served by Webster) 19:58

Shots on Goal					
	Canada	10	8	6	24
	Russia	10	12	8	30

LEADING SCORERS

	G	A	PTS
Bobby Hull, Canada	7	2	9
Gordie Howe, Canada	3	5	8
Alexander Yakushev, USSR	6	1	7
Andre Lacroix, Canada	1	6	7
Vladimir Petrov, USSR	1	6	7
Ralph Backstrom, Canada	4	2	6
Boris Mikhailov, USSR	4	2	6
Vladimir Shadrin, USSR	2	4	6
Mark Howe, Canada	2	3	5
J. C. Tremblay, Canada	1	4	5
Alexander Gusev, USSR	3	1	4
Alexander Maltsev, USSR	4	0	4
Yuri Lebedev, USSR	2	2	4
Vyacheslav Anisin, USSR	2	2	4
Paul Henderson, Canada	2	1	3
Tom Webster, Canada	2	1	3
Vladimir Vikulov, USSR	0	3	3
Bruce MacGregor, Canada	1	1	2
Frank Mahovlich, Canada	1	1	2